The Letters of John Cowper Powys to G.R. Wilson Knight

EDITED BY
ROBERT BLACKMORE

CECIL WOOLF · LONDON

First published 1983
Letters © Francis L. Powys, 1983
Introduction, Editorial Notes and Appendix 4 © Robert Blackmore, 1983. 'Cosmic Correspondences' and letter to the Nobel Committee of the Swedish Academy © G. Wilson Knight, 1983. 'World Famous Writer Returns to Scholar' © 'Psychic News', 1963, 1983

Cecil Woolf Publishers, 1 Mornington Place, London NW1 7RP
Tel: 01-387 2394

ISBN 0-900821-48-5

Contents

Introduction	*page* 7
Editorial Note	22
I The Start of the Correspondence, 1937-1949	25
II Letters from Corwen, 1950-April 1955	38
III Letters from Blaenau Ffestiniog, May 1955-February 1957	57
IV Letters from Blaenau Ffestiniog, May 1957-December 1957	73
V The Last Letters, 1958-1962	95
Notes	111
Appendix 1: Cosmic Correspondences by G. Wilson Knight	117
Appendix 2: G. Wilson Knight's letter nominating John Cowper Powys for the Nobel Prize	130
Appendix 3: 'World-Famous Writer Returns to Scholar'	133
Appendix 4: Major Publications by John Cowper Powys and G. Wilson Knight, 1932-1962	136
Index	138

Illustrations

Between pages 80 and 81

1. John Cowper Powys in the late 1950s at 1 Waterloo, Blaenau Ffestiniog. Kenneth Hopkins Collection
2. John Cowper Powys in the 1960s at 1 Waterloo, Blaenau Ffestiniog. Kenneth Hopkins Collection
3. John Cowper Powys in the 1930s at Rats Barn, East Chaldon, Dorset. Kenneth Hopkins Collection
4. G. Wilson Knight in 1955. Courtesy of 'The Yorkshire Post'
5. G. Wilson Knight in the role of Timon of Athens, at the Hart House Theatre, Toronto, February 1940. Sent to Powys by Knight in December 1956. Photograph by C. Sauerbrei

Introduction

Fifty letters from one of the century's most provocative authors to one of its most distinguished critics. Fifty letters written from the author's sixty-fifth to his ninetieth year, 1937 to 1962.

Serious students of twentieth-century literature need nothing further: here are all John Cowper Powys's words to G. Wilson Knight. Excerpts from the letters have appeared in several books and journals during the past decade, provoking, always, a wide range of responses. Certainly it is time to forego excerpts, time to look fully at the letters within the context of everything that Powys had to say to Knight about literature, death, second childhood, and—at the centre of the controversy— masturbation.

Casual readers of literature, however, may know little more of Knight and Powys than the generous quotations from Knight's books of Shakespearian interpretation which appear in virtually every new work about Shakespeare; and such often-quoted praise of Powys as Angus Wilson's 'There is little doubt that he will stand with James, Lawrence, and Joyce in the eyes of future critics' and Henry Miller's 'Powys's *Autobiography* I still believe to be the greatest, the most magnificent of all autobiographies'. Précising lives so rich as Powys's and Knight's is hardly possible, but these notes can provide some signal facts.

John Cowper Powys's publishing career extended over sixty-five years. Although his primary works appeared in the decade before and the decade after World War Two, his first volume arrived in 1895 and his last in 1960, during his eighty-eighth year. And three short novels written after that have been published by Village Press, London, in 1974-75. Born in 1872—ten and thirteen years before James Joyce and D.H. Lawrence—he was the eldest of eleven children born to a Church of England Vicar and his brooding, book-loving wife; seven of the ten children who lived to adulthood wrote books, and an eighth, the eldest daughter, was a painter. After finishing at Corpus Christi College, Cambridge, Powys earned his living for more than thirty years by lecturing about literature, first in England and then, between 1905 and 1930, in America where—before television and the wide popularity of radio and cinema—the lecture platforms of the cities and towns served a significant cultural and social function. During countless hours on trains and in the hotel rooms of the United States and Canada, Powys wrote regularly, but not until the simultaneous success of two books in 1929—*The Meaning of Culture* and his fourth-published novel, *Wolf Solent*—could he afford to give full time to writing. After four most prolific years in a secluded farm cottage in New York State, he returned to Britain—first to Dorset and then, in 1935, to North Wales. Powys's last thirty years stand in sharpest contrast to his earlier life. The speaking tours, he said, took him across the Atlantic sixty times and into all but two of the forty-eight states; in rural New York and in Wales he rarely went more than three miles from home on his daily two-hour walks.

Powys's masterpieces are *A Glastonbury Romance*

INTRODUCTION

(1932), the *Autobiography* (1934), *Porius* (1951), and, I believe, his letters—those already published and the volumes that will follow. Letters, a dying art, perhaps, in a time of instant visual communication and swift travel, are the articulate and unrehearsed (at least for Powys) written discourse to an audience of one that occasionally, with people of strong personalities and spontaneous spirits, become literature for all. Powys, preeminently, is one whose written conversations not only serve to complement his essays and novels, but stand greatly alone as the presentation of a character—or characters—named Powys. *Characters* is the truer word. And Powys well knew that he cast himself in various roles for his many correspondents. Writing to his friend Louis Wilkinson about a proposed biography of his brother Llewelyn (nicknamed 'Lulu') he said,

> but of course we are all of us so very different according to the person we're with . . . there's Lulu to me—Lulu to you—Lulu to ——, to ——, to ——, to ——. At least a dozen Lulus, & then *finally* there is Lulu *to* Lulu. [The omission of names is Powys's.]

Phyllis Playter—who by sharing the last forty years of his life knew Powys best—is correct in her hope that there will be a collection of his letters to a wide range of correspondents that will give a well-rounded portrait of Powys. And yet there is continuing need for the entire correspondence to a single recipient that avoids the inevitable distortion of selected publication where, quite naturally, an editor chooses the most interesting letters and those that best document his own feelings about the writer. Selection, by excluding the petty, the pedestrian, the redundant—and sometimes the controversial—while preserving the most inspired letters, paints too glamorous a picture. But a total run of letters such as this, although presenting only the face that Powys prepared for Knight, can serve as a series of still photographs snapped from a single vantage point over a quarter of a century. Rather than a posed-by-the-editor portrait, we may see a more real person moving through time.

The letters to G. Wilson Knight show Powys playing for an academic audience. A letter to Wilkinson about Knight's April 2, 1957, visit suggests Powys's attitude towards teachers. 'We are expecting a visit from Professor Knight of Leeds on Tuesday, so I must play the Fool tomorrow so unlimitedly that I shall be good and quiet on April 2.' In letters to friends, Powys always referred to Knight as the Professor and spoke often of his demanding professional eyes. On January 29th of the same year he wrote to Wilkinson,

> Our Leeds Professor G. Wilson Knight has been getting good reviews for his Byron [*Lord Byron's Marriage*]. . . . Prof. Knight is a good detective and I've known about him ever since he visited us in Corwen. He has the most piercing turnscrew gimlety eyes you ever saw in your life. How scared his pupils in Leeds must be of him.

The quality of a correspondence depends on the quality of the writer's heart and mind, and, perhaps less obviously, on those of the recipient. Among the many hundreds of people to whom Powys wrote (he wrote up-

INTRODUCTION

wards of 40,000 letters during the 33,000 days of his life: he speaks of writing seventeen letters one day, twenty on another, and he rarely failed to answer even a stranger's note), Knight proved an ideal correspondent in many ways. A brief introduction can give only hints toward the rich complexity of G. Wilson Knight's approaches to life and literature and theatre, but, fortunately, the full tellings of his mind are available in all good libraries—his works on Shakespeare and Byron, certainly, and perhaps his interpretations of Pope, the Romantic Poets, British drama, and his autobiographical writings. In the Appendix to these letters are three documents by Knight, including his nomination of Powys for the Nobel Prize in Literature. And it is but twelve years since the publication of his *Neglected Powers*, a collection of essays that bring to fullest conclusions the long and consistent development of his ideas over the more than forty years since their first presentation in *Myth and Miracle* (1929) and *The Wheel of Fire* (1930). *Neglected Powers* (1971) contains the essays on Francis Berry and 'The Scholar Gipsy' discussed in these letters, and five chapters about Powys. These chapters, together with Knight's *The Saturnian Quest* (1964), constitute the first and richest study-in-depth of John Cowper Powys's novels and poetry, studies to which all future considerations must turn.

Born in Surrey, the younger of two sons of George and Caroline Knight, George Wilson Knight was educated at Dulwich College and St Edmund Hall, Oxford, served as a motorcycle dispatch rider in the near-East during World War One, and taught at Dean Close School, Cheltenham, until his appointment in 1931 as Chancellors' Professor of English at Trinity College in the University of Toronto. Nine years later, with the war making it impossible to spend his summers in England with his mother and his brother, W.F. Jackson Knight, the distinguished classicist, Knight returned to England, first as a master at Stowe, and then to the University of Leeds from which he retired, as Professor of English Literature, in 1962. His teaching appointments conceal, however, that the theatre—acting, producing, directing, playwriting—evoked his strongest loyalties. When made a Commander of the Order of the British Empire in 1968, Wilson Knight attributed the honour as much to his theatrical contributions as to his teaching career and his more than thirty books. At Cheltenham, Toronto, Leeds, and—in 1941—in London, Knight's productions of and performances in Shakespearian dramas (Timon of Athens is his most noted part) have reflected the strong aesthetic and interpretative beliefs presented most fully in his *Shakespearian Production* (1964). Living now in Exeter, he continues to write about literature, Spiritualism, his brother (*Jackson Knight: A Biography*, Alden Press, Oxford, 1975), and, on occasion, to lecture. In the spring of 1974, Knight's lectures on Shakespeare at many of Canada's leading universities proved a happy return a third of a century after his resignation from the University of Toronto.

 John Cowper Powys and G. Wilson Knight met only four times: the three brief visits discussed in these letters and a call of homage during Powys's last months when, beyond speech in the spring of his ninety-first year, he confirmed by gesture his essential agreements with Knight,

INTRODUCTION

and gave silent benediction. The entire body of Powys's friendship is preserved in these letters. Unlike most human relationships where much happens during personal meetings and goes unrecorded, here, fully transcribed, are all the themes and variations—marred only by the loss of Knight's letters. His words in the Appendix serve as partial fill-ins.

Powys knew from Knight's initial letter that they had much in common, 'as far as I can at present sound your mind'. There were the obvious similarities between two men born during Queen Victoria's reign and educated at Cambridge or Oxford who had committed themselves greatly to the creation and criticism of literature. (Among Powys's fifty-odd books are eight of criticism, including the important studies, *Rabelais, Dostoievsky,* and *Dorothy M. Richardson.*) The deeper parallels involve life's ultimate questions—Powys questing back towards the First Cause and Knight pressing forward through Spiritualism—as they sought the why-whence-whithers of man's existence, and the recognition by each that he was, essentially, an actor. Both will survive through their books, but each, in England and during long expatriations in North America, earned his way on the lecture platform or at the classroom lectern. Powys and Knight seemed to feel most effective while using the sounds of words, the gestures of public presentation, the range of subtleties possible in person but unavailable with a reader. Indeed, neither author is a great stylist. The writings of both—Powys through his often formless, underscored extensions and Knight with his complex cross-referencing—suggest impatience with the capabilities of the printed word. As poet and dramatist each remains little known.

Powys's letters abound in statements confessing his view of himself as an actor—an endowment he finds almost inborn. 'There is no use trying to conceal the fact that Nature from the start had made me an actor,' he says in the *Autobiography*. 'In my extreme infancy at Shirley I acted the part of my Father in the Pulpit, although I cannot remember ever seeing him in the Shirley pulpit.' And Knight's still-to-be-published *Symbol of Man*—the text illustrated with near-nude photographs of prototypal gestures, stances, and physical attitudes for which Knight himself posed—remains for the author one of the prime expressions of what he has to tell us about mankind.

Both of these post-Darwinian questers turned often to a book published the year Powys was born, Nietzsche's *The Birth of Tragedy*, and both are 'Dionysian'. In his essay on Arnold's 'The Scholar Gipsy' Knight writes, 'Our consciousness has become, to use Nietzsche's terms, too purely "Apollonian," too heated, and needs fertilization again from the cool depths of the "Dionysian," the more darkly feminine, and eastern powers.' And more than once Knight has quoted approvingly Nietzsche's 'to the knower all instincts are hallowed' and 'Once hadst thou passions and calledst them evil. Now hast thou only thy virtues; they grew out of thy passions.' In *The Pleasures of Literature* [*The Enjoyment of Literature* in the U.S.] Powys advises that, although we need not accept any of Nietzsche's doctrines, 'what *is* essential, if we are not . . . to stop our ears to the most prophetic voice since Blake, is that we should apply to the spiritual drama of our own life the searching psychology Nietzsche applied to his'. The same essay contradicts some of the counsel that his father the Vicar continued to preach[1] until Powys was in his middle years:

> But the ideal of our Western humanity under the influence of Christianity has corrupted this healthy belligerency. A set of unnatural values has appeared, begotten upon the sick, perverse, morbid instincts of the enslaved masses by crafty priests and nature-hating prophets, values that place the human ideal in 'another,' a 'better' world, values that treat as 'evil' the three most beautiful things in life—voluptuousness, passion-for-power, and courageous selfishness.
>
> 'Good,' according to this 'slave-morality,' is to be loving to one's neighbour *so that he shall love us in return*; to repress sexual voluptuousness so as to poison the natural happiness of the beautiful and the brave; and to despise the body for the sake of the 'spirit,' so that our weakness and 'unselfishness' shall perpetuate humanity *as it is*. (543-4)

Powys and Knight have been essentially alone in their questings. No coteries grew round them as each pressed beyond the old codes and rationalities. Both have been much out of fashion, standing staunchly apart from the century's publicized literary movements. Stubbornly pursuing their own answers by their own best inner lights—by the sanctity of their own instincts and imaginations—both learned to accept psychological obsessions in their own makeups, and, by the very act of open acceptance, found strengthened creative energies. G. Wilson Knight diagnoses himself as an exhibitionist, and his April, 1974, letter which introduces the next chapter gives his understanding of his own obsession, and discusses Powys's sadism.

The most casual reader of Powys soon finds the preoccupation with sadism that Powys saw as the root of his sexuality (and close to the core of his being), and may well wonder whether the *Autobiography* is accurate in reporting that there were but three specific acts of cruelty—all quite trivial to citizens of a century that has given us the Holocaust and glibly assigns the initials S-M to our nicer sadistic-masochistic doings. The grossest of the three youthful acts—chopping up earthworms and putting their parts in a fountain while his family was at church—may only hint, it might seem, at direr actions. But a reading of Powys's works and thousands of his unpublished and unusually frank letters indicates that he *did* nothing more than dissect live worms. (Powys became the most ardent of anti-vivisectionists.) All the rest of his sadism was fantasized, and, although in some codes the thought is as bad as the deed, imagined cruelties have no victims. The truth seems to be that Powys used sadistic thoughts for sexual arousal, sometimes with the help of 'forbidden books available only from Paris'. And only after excrutiating early struggles with his Victorian-bred conscience was he able to accept— and sublimate—what he had found perverse.

'Endure and enjoy,' Wolf Solent and others of his fictional characters learn, but nowhere during his lifetime was Powys able to publish fully the masturbatory

INTRODUCTION

aspects of the matter. There are broad suggestions in the first chapter of the *Autobiography* and two brief sentences in *All or Nothing* (1960) that endorse the 'important and creative act'. But in these letters to Knight he stresses the efficacy of onanism, its capacity for reducing evil in the world, and the need for Knight to become an open advocate. These are not new thoughts for Powys; in 1923, in a long letter[2] responding to accusations by his brother Llewelyn, he wrote in part:

> I grant the 'onanism,' I confess to the 'self-abuse,' the spiritual 'shagging,' but these things may have more mysteries & wonders in them than you can guess. At any rate I am resolute to defend it. You do not succeed in making me ashamed . . . except of giving the Maberlulu[3] a chance of jeering! . . . I would like to write an essay on this subject & *maybe I will*. God! I could.
>
> If you think its an unreal thing, an unauthentic thing, a kind of pose—you're absolutely wrong. One doesn't pose when one—I need not repeat the expressive 'Prep.' word! It can't be *both* unreal *and* disgusting you know—its either one or the other—. But Nature made me—& to her I appeal—I appeal to Caesar like poor Paul before Festus—. And if Nature makes a feeling thrilling & lovely to me . . . why should I try & suppress it because Lulu calls it 'aesthetically unpleasing'? Perhaps its no more aesthetically unpleasing to Nature than Bill Pod's encounters with his Suffolk goat!
>
> Lulu you are an aesthetic tyrant; & your severe

aestheticism is damned like the old 'morality' writ large! [....]

But don't you see I *am* an epicene queer abnormal pervert in *everything*—when I write poetry I 'make love' in my 'unpleasing' way . . . when I walk on the hills .. the same! by the sea .. the same! when I drink coffee .. the same! and I don't 'cheapen' or 'vulgarize' these things! It is the Moon *'in trine'* with Venus, I expect, in my horoscope .. and this isn't a pose—but I am humbly obstinately just so! My whole life is 'exaggerated' in this sense .. I am a born perverted sensationalist—I *like* 'prostituting' my imagination the sweet bitch!—what else is she for? [....]

Is all the world to be exactly like Lulu? I don't attack *you* for your essential peculiarities! But I am grateful for the opportunity you give me to re-consider the whole matter—and I'm damned if I *want* to change —After all Nature puts her seal on what is best for each of us by the mystery of the *happiness* that such things bring—and if I feel *very* happy in my onanistic abandonments; if I feel absolutely thrilled with delicious magical secret lovely happiness when I 'talk' of themselves to my girls and make idols and fetishes and funny little worshipped stocks & stones of them and find all the mystery of Nature in them—well! who can blame?

I refuse to obey any aesthetic rules *or* moral rules *or* philosophic rules as to my life—. If Nature has made certain emotions wonderful to me .. well then . . . let her justify me! She'll see to it that they don't cheapen or vulgarize anything . . . What cheapens & vulgarizes

INTRODUCTION

is the untrue, the unreal, the false, the conventional—and it would *be* false and conventional for me to try to pose as a cynical and worldly wise philosopher.

It is perhaps unfortunate that Powys did not write—or could not then publish—the proposed article at that time. In the single decade since his death the world has opened greatly. Indeed, youth of today may little understand the suppressive forces that imposed taboos on such actions—and topics—as masturbation and public nudity. In the spring of 1974, came the fad of running naked through the streets, the auditoriums, the public places of the world, and the striking change was not in the act but in the easy acceptance of it by most age groups and social classes. With tolerant humour and with a healthy minimum of voyeurism, most people accepted the exhibitionism so benignly that the 'streakers' often seemed deprived of the joy of shocking.

Masturbation, too, has emerged so rapidly from the shadows that the issue of *Time Magazine* for 1 April 1974 casually carried into nearly five million households news about one of the clinics of the University of California Medical School in San Francisco:

> Depending on their problems, clients (the word 'patient' is never used) have a full curriculum of programs from which to choose. For 'pre-orgasmic' women (those who have never achieved orgasm), there is a ten-session course in which they discuss their problems with female counselors, view movies, and receive homework assignments in such subjects as masturbation technique and use of fantasy in sex. Of the 150

women who have taken this program, 90% were eventually able to achieve orgasm.

Can a young person today measure the sheer daring of a discussion of masturbation by men born into Victorian times when there was wide-spread belief that insane asylums were largely kept full by those who had indulged in—to use a Victorian phrase—self-abuse? Perhaps D.H. Lawrence's outdated words can suggest the measure of the ancient taboo and how short the time since its passing—words written the year before his death and the year after *Lady Chatterly's Lover* was found so sexually audacious that it had to be privately printed in Italy:

> [Masturbation] always carries this secret feeling of futility and humiliation . . . . And this is, perhaps, the deepest and most dangerous cancer of our civilization. Instead of being a pure and harmless vice, masturbation is certainly the most dangerous sexual vice that a society can be inflicted with, in the long run. (*Pornography and Obscenity*, 1929, p. 19)

Opinion has changed radically, but on one topic Lawrence spoke for the majority—in 1929.

The letters from John Cowper Powys to G. Wilson Knight range wide over the subjects that concern literate citizens of any age, clime, or persuasion, with the emphasis, always, on the positive and the creative. For both men, the heart and the instincts take precedence over the head. Both prefer acceptance to rejection, and both see a multiverse as the stage for man. Powys was fond of an adjective (and perhaps played on its sound in naming his novel *Porius*) that is appropriate for both Powys and

INTRODUCTION

Knight, and for the generations emerging during the last quarter of the twentieth century. No thoughtful viewer or creative interpreter of man's role and destiny can bring a closed mind to his thinking, to his living. Powys and Knight—each in his own way—remain always open, remain, in Powys's word, *porous*.

Powys's *Autobiography* covers only his first sixty years. The final third of his life is recorded in his letters. The fifty written to Knight from 1937 to 1962 serve as one chapter—the side of himself he chose to talk out with 'the Professor from Leeds'. These, together with letters to others now in print or scheduled for publication, compose the second part of John Cowper Powys's autobiography.

R. L. B.

Editorial Note

The primary editorial intention is to let John Cowper Powys's letters speak for themselves. The interruptions are as unobtrusive as I can make them: when few words suffice, they are incorporated within square brackets in the text as little more disruptive than the symbol for a footnote; footnotes carry the longer clarifications, while brief chapter introductions provide the more general background information. But more often than not, Powys will identify people and places later in a letter, if not at first mention. And I have not disrupted the flow of the written conversation to provide information available, for those who wish it, in standard reference sources.

The transcription of these letters—written very rapidly, the handwriting often suggests—is as exact as I can make it. Misspellings and solecisms are preserved, and inconsistencies of punctuation remain as written (*don't* and *dont* may appear in the same paragraph). It is possible that some of Powys's variants held meaning for him; a tidy editor making silent corrections becomes a destroyer of evidence. All these matters stand without the chidings that the repeated word *sic* would bring.

Powys was fond of dots . . . between phrases and sentences. These are preserved, and should never be taken as elipses indicating deletion from his letters. No word that he wrote to Knight is omitted.

Powys's penchant for multiple underscoring—sometimes as many as seven lines slashed under a phrase—

EDITORIAL NOTE

poses a typographic challenge. I use italics to indicate one or two lines under the words; bold type signals three or more emphatic underlinings.

Because Powys lived in but two places during the correspondence—Corwen, North Wales, until May 1955, and Blaenau Ffestiniog, some forty miles west of Corwen, during his last eight years—his carefully inscribed return addresses are not recorded after the first three letters. There are no other omissions.

Three libraries make possible this publication: the letters themselves are in the Brotherton Collection at the University of Leeds, while the magnificent Powys collections in the Humanities Research Center of The University of Texas, Austin, and the Colgate University Library, Hamilton, New York, furnished most of the supplementary information. Libraries are but stone and steel, however, thus my true appreciation goes to David I. Masson at Leeds, whom I met only through correspondence; and to F. Warren Roberts, Director of the Humanities Research Center, and Bruce M. Brown, Colgate University Librarian, for their personal courtesies and those of their staffs. With their permission I use quotations from Powys's letter to his brother Llewelyn, at Texas, and his letters to Louis Wilkinson, at Colgate. A grant from the Colgate University Research Council provided my travelling expenses to Texas.

Like all who write about John Cowper Powys, I am indebted to Francis Powys, his nephew and literary executor, to the late Laurence Pollinger, his agent throughout much of his publishing career, and to Gerald Pollinger who carries on the family tradition of enlightened literary business management. Once again it is a pleasant duty to acknowledge their permissions and a most welcome opportunity to thank them for all that they continue to do to facilitate Powys scholarship. And although she was not involved in this project, the late Miss Phyllis Playter--resident, until her death on 10 March 1982, at 1 Waterloo, Blaenau Ffestiniog—warrants a posthumous, eternal and heartfelt thank-you from all who knew Powys and all who relish his words.

My primary debt of gratitude is, of course, to Wilson Knight whose generous replies to my queries are so much in keeping with his dedicated service to literature for more than half a century. As these letters go off to the publishers, I learn from Professor Knight that he has decided to accept the advice Powys gives in this correspondence, and will now officially be called *Richard*. The text will stand as written, but let the closing salute go to G. Richard Wilson Knight.

R. L. B.

I
The Start of the Correspondence
1937-1949

In the summer of 1937, John Cowper Powys was visiting his brother and sisters in Dorset when G. Wilson Knight wrote from Cheltenham to offer copies of his Atlantic Crossing *and* The Christian Renaissance. *Knight's letters were not saved, but a letter to me in April 1974 recalls his initiation of the correspondence thirty-seven years earlier*:

You ask me what prompted me to write to Powys. As far as I remember, I wrote after reading *A Glastonbury Romance* in the summer of 1937. I had some years before that bought and started *Wolf Solent*, but had not finished it. I found it rather heavy going, and stopped after reading a half or two thirds, and failed to continue. When I mentioned J.C. Powys's books in *Atlantic Crossing* (p. 295) in 1936, I was thinking mainly of *Wolf Solent*. I bought *A Glastonbury Romance* when it appeared in 1933, but was afraid of its length, and I think also of its challenging contents, of which I may have been aware from glancing through it, since my reference in *Atlantic Crossing* uses the plural ('books'). I then put it aside for some three or four years, attacking it seriously in 1936 or 1937. In *The Burning Oracle* (1939, p. 292) I referred to *A Glastonbury Romance* as 'perhaps the greatest work of our generation'.

I was quite overpowered by its beauty and splendour of writing, its range of sexual and mystical insights, its occult perceptions, and above all by the study of Mr Evans's sadistic obsession. I say 'above all', because this had a personal interest for me.

My own interest in the physical body was being developed at this time into the acting of parts in semi-nudity; you can see pictures of them in my *Shakespearian Production*, pictures 15, 16, 19, 20, and frontispiece (32 in paperback); they are, of the Messenger in *Antony and Cleopatra*, 1937; Caliban, 1938; and Timon, early in 1940, my usual Autumn production having been delayed. I had a try-out of the Messenger scenes early in 1937, the full production following in the autumn. Nudity was not so acceptable then as now, and it took some courage for a well-known person in his own circle to develop it within his own productions.

I was given confidence so to engage myself by my recent reading of Nietzsche's *Thus Spake Zarathustra*, in which I sensed again and again a relevant doctrine concerning the acceptance of implanted instinct (see my *Neglected Powers*, pp. 171-8), which I grouped with Pope's doctrine of instinct and the 'ruling passion' in his *Essay on Man* and *Moral Essays* (the one to Cobham; *Neglected Powers*, pp. 170-1). I also about this time began to see that this drive had been behind all my interest in the stage and acting from an early age. There had been in the past some danger from it, and there was still much attendant anxiety, but I knew that, as Nietzsche puts it, 'Hitherto hath all knowledge grown up with an evil conscience' (*Zarathustra*, III, 12; *Neglected Powers*,

p. 172); and so I deliberately decided to go, step by step, ahead. I felt myself both guided and guarded.

The description of Mr Evans's experience corresponded, point by point, with my own; especially at that moment when, his whole self once set deliberately on the course of daring, physical quiescence results (*A Glastonbury Romance*, XXIX, 1051 or 1004; *Neglected Powers*, p. 160). Of this I had myself been aware in the try-out Messenger scenes, when the actual performance drew near. And there was so much else, including the stated fact that what was happening was characterized less by pleasure than by a fearful obedience, though the will to satisfaction had prompted it (*A Glastonbury Romance*, XXIX, 1060 or 1012; *Neglected Powers*, pp. 159-60). I knew it all so well. Though the purposes were of a different kind, their functioning corresponded.

I expect it was this primarily that made me write to Powys, and I may have hinted at my own experience as resembling his study; or I may have been thinking of his *Autobiography* too, if I had read it by then. This would account for his saying that we had something in common.

From 1937 on, I followed up with Caliban in 1938 and Timon in 1940. I had been leading up to Timon as my main contribution in this line, and in doing it with considerable acclaim (as my reviews show), I have always felt that I was, in my own small way, living Nietzsche's words:

> Thou goest thy way of greatness; now is that become thy final refuge which hath been hitherto thine extremest peril. (*Zarathustra*, III, 1; *Neglected Powers*, p. 349)

I did the relevant scenes in London, at the Westminster Theatre, in 1941 (*Shakespearian Production*, p. 314), and the whole play at Leeds in 1948; each time with complete success.[4] The only aspersion on my Timon as an exhibitionist act came in a letter from a stranger in 1941 during *This Sceptred Isle,* accusing me of turning the theatre into a 'psychiatric clinic'. This I take to be, everything considered, the most important creative contribution of my life. My 'devils', as Nietzsche has it, had become 'angels' (*Zarathustra*, I. 5; *Neglected Powers*, p. 174). I should here emphasize that my following of Pope and Nietzsche has not been just a matter of *thinking*, but an engagement far more strenuous and demanding, involving *action*.

The modern stage has developed nudity to an extreme, sometimes well and sometimes not so well; and this whole movement may be related to my early (1940) essay 'The Body Histrionic', now in *Shakespearian Production*; and also to my as yet unpublished *Symbol of Man*, which I regard as my central work.

In social affairs, I show the extreme of non-exhibitionist behaviour. I dislike dressing up and am retiring in manner. In my garden, I wear a minimum of clothes in summer. My obsession responds, as did Timon, to the Sun.

Exeter, 1974. *   G. Wilson Knight

*With minor corrections in 1977. During the past three years Prof. Knight has performed in a one-man dramatic recital on stages in North America and England, taking the roles of Lear, Timon, Caliban, and others. His latest book, *Shakespeare's Dramatic Challenge* (London, Croom Helm, 1977), takes its title from the recital and includes a discussion of it.

THE START OF THE CORRESPONDENCE

Thus it was that an actor-professor-critic in his late thirties, caught up by the insights he found in A Glastonbury Romance *during a crucial period in his own inner development, initiated correspondence with the author he was not to meet till many years later. It is unfortunate that we do not have his side of the exchange, but Powys's custom of prompt and specific response to the letter just received serves quite well to fill the gaps.*

I

3 East Chaldon, Dorchester, Dorset.
July 27 1937.

Dear Mr Knight

I am *greatly* interested in your letter & I w^d indeed be *very* grateful to you if you would really send me *both* these books: both The Transatlantic Journey and The Christian Renaissance.

I am proud & pleased at your thought of including a study of my Glastonbury in anything you write; for as far as I can *at present* sound your mind it seems that we have a lot in common.

I shall be here till Aug 4 or 5 when I return to
          Corwen
          Merionethshire
          North Wales.

I am enjoying quite a 'vita nuova' by my plunge into my ancestral principality.

                              Yrs v sincerely
                              J.C. Powys.

2

East Chaldon, Dorchester, Dorset.
July 30 1937.

Dear Mr Wilson Knight

Thank you a lot for sending me so promptly your 'Atlantic Crossing' & giving me the hope of ere long receiving the other too.

I've got a book of essays [*The Pleasures of Literature*] to finish before I can do justice to your two books; but perhaps this is just as well as the unavoidable delay will enable me to read the two books one after another & thus be in a position to describe to you my reactions to your work & to your ideas with fuller material before me.

I don't leave for Wales
7 Cae Coed
Corwen
Merionethshire
till Aug 6th.

I glanced at the close of your book & quickly perceived that I have never done justice to your Cheltenham and its environs.

Yrs v sincerely
John Cowper Powys

P.S. I was glad to see your picture in this book.

THE START OF THE CORRESPONDENCE

3

7 Cae Coed, Corwen, Merionethshire, N. Wales.
Sept 5 1941.

Dear Mr Knight

Please forgive this disgraceful gap between *Aug 29 & Sept 5!* But I over-worked my eyes[1] a trifle & have had to cut down a bit in my letter-writing—tho' letters (both ways) are a great delight to me & (on *my* side) a positive *Vice!*

But I am *so* pleased to hear from you and I am proud of the way you bring me in this remarkable powerful & penetrating essay on our friend Berry's poetry.[2] I am so thankful to learn from you that he is still alive.

I have *still got*, I believe, *the MSS* of his *Fall of a Tower* which I admire greatly & wrote to him about. He sent it to me more than a year ago (it must be it came from Cheltenham) and I was fearful lest he had been killed as I'd heard no more—but *thank the Lord* your words in *this printed note* re-assure me about his fate.

Tis nice to think you have come to England for good now.

Yrs most sincerely
J.C. Powys.

4

March 3 1942.

Dear Professor Knight

I thank you very much for getting your Publisher

to send me this copy of the 'Starlit Dome.' The one in it I like the *best*, 'by *a long shot*,' *so far* is the one **on Keats** and I am sure Keats is a much *severer test*—(tho' that word sounds odd when applied to the most sensuous & voluptuous and, as you well say, most *'rounded'* poetry of the three poets here)—of a real personal response to the secrets of poetry as poetry *than the other three* you deal with in this book. The mere fact that in the case of Keats the Interpreter cannot digress down various attractive by-alleys and by-vistas of speculation or doctrine in *itself makes it more* of an ordeal. He is compelled to *hover close* over the actual shapes colours motions and fragrances—yes! & imponderable emanations reaching us thro' the pores of our skins as it were—of the **words themselves.** He *cannot fly off & be still dealing* with the subject.

Alas! I mustn't write more: *for my eyes* have become rather a hypochondriacal care to me this year and I *have* (even rather churlishly I fear sometimes) to save them for earning my living! But I do thank you, Professor, for this book.

Yrs v. sincerely
J.C. Powys.

5

November 2 1948.

My dear Professor

O no! I swear across my heart I *didn't glance* at the index and I can also swear with absolute truth that

THE START OF THE CORRESPONDENCE

I was far more interested in the most *G. Wilson Knight parts* of the book [*Christ and Nietzsche*]—for in this sort of approach (w^h we share, I can see, and practice in common) what is alluring and rewarding is *not* what you can supply for yourself but what *another* buccaneer of the spirit, or *another* pirate-ship, can capture from the great galleons from the Isles of Gold. Our method is really the same only we steer of course—& properly & naturally and boldly so—*on our own steam* or *with our own chart* or whatever you call that thing they use to steer by the heavens (not merely *compass*) quadrant is it or 'astrolobe' or something—I forget! but never mind the thing 'they' use . . . What you & I, my dear professor, use is our own particular *'soul entire'* and not any specialized portion of it!

No I found your book—& I find all the echoes of your work I meet with—& I wholly agree about the poetry of our mutual friend Berry—of the *same atmosphere* or mental chemistry as the one wherein I breathe most freely & from which I draw my best bouts of life-force. Are you a brother, Professor, of the Knight who wrote on Vergil?? Wasn't it called Roman Vergil?[3]

No no! I have just this very day got your good cash from my agents as the Cassell accounts come round & I think on the contrary you were *very generous* to *pay so much.* I love your praise my friend but I have a queer mania I suppose a *'complex'* but as I am my own psychologist I don't know for sure *whether its what they call that,* but *I* call my mania *'anti-narcissism'* & for all I know you may share it for I can see that I am also like you in cultivating (anyway as thinker & critic) the delicate

C

& difficult art of being humble-minded for (like you) I have discovered that humility not the christian sort but a quite heathen sort is one of the best *'organa'* of research you can possibly have—but this anti-narcissism of mine is different from humility—it is as I say a very odd inhibition—I mean **I can't bear** *reading any words of my own! Once they are safe in print* I don't want to think of them!! But on the other hand I dont at all like *not* getting what I've writ **printed!**

You've beaten me totally, Knight, over *Timon*. Tis *a play I hardly have read at all*[4] & I could not tell you why for I simply don't **know** why! But I love to have and see your picture as an actor; for *there we are very much at one.* I always used to *interpret best as an actor* in my lectures; by *Acting Shakespeare's words much more* than by words of my own.

Well I must stop—I say! but *what* a lot of books on Dostoievsky are coming out!

Yrs very gratefully
J.C. Powys

[*on the envelope*]

There is a *tremendous need* at this moment of our history for this book 'Christ and Nietzsche'—

The more I read it—totally & scrupulously & even neurotically (owing to my anti-narcisstic complex) dodging *all* your allusions to that 'militant degenerate' masquerading as the champion of the *'Common man'* your fellow-actor J.C.P.—the more I like it & the more I find I agree with you. You & I, my dear Knight, are certainly very like each other & our *destiny* from the old world to new and back again are alike!

THE START OF THE CORRESPONDENCE

6

March 29 1949.

My dear Knight

Sure it'll be *very* nice to see you Saturday April 23, St Georges Day & Sun rises at 4-49 says my Diary. So it'll be shining full into *this room* when you are seated in my grey guest-chair with your head against my favourite volumes!

I can tell you the way myself! Turn to *your right* when you come out of the station and take a rough path on your left up the *side of a hill* where the trees have been *all lately cut down!* There are 2 paths to the left going up this hill but the one for you is the one that *follows along the course of road and railway and river too only at a mounting level* but *following the course of the railway as it goes West to Bala! Then* at last you will come to 22 stone steps & then turn to right & do *not* go to the *'Council Houses'* but go on for 300 or 400 yards along the road (still West) to *CAE COED.*

When you at last *really get to Cae Coed* you can either come *up the lane* to the second iron gate and ours is the *last but one house*; or come up the *little main front drive*!

Well so long till April *23* about 3.30 I *expect.*

Yrs
J C Powys

7

May 6 1949.

Forgive me for disobeying you my dear friend but I have read enough already in both the chapter called 'New Testament as an Art Form' & the one called 'Mankind in Glory an Essay on St Paul' [in *The Christian Renaissance*] to find out how *exactly* the quality of your thought & imagination suits me & goes along on parallel lines with my own thought & imagination. *We sure are a pair* you & I (or me?) just like the two wheels of Elijah's chariot or the 2 horses (of course the 2 *immortal* ones!) of that Homeric chariot—Achilles's was it?—that poor Master Camerado P. borrowed to go at Hector in—& *never came back*! or like 2 horns of *some* Horned God, I forget which particular one, but they *'most all'* had a *tendency* to grow them (I don't refer to the sort Panurge had such a dislike of!)

No but seriously my dear friend I have constantly been telling my American lady how I regard your visit as a Red Letter Day in these latter years—(I wont say 'a gala night in these *lonesome latter years*' because my Phyllis for all being 22 years younger is such a perfect critical help to me in all I think feel invent & write. Well! *you'll see her* on *your next visit* w^h I pray won't be too long deferred my friend)

Never mind about those old leaflets boosting the Autobiography—but seriously I am made very grateful by what you say about helping me over any book or translation *on* or *of Aristophanes*, & I do love the *particular way* you bring in your brother—that attitude of

THE START OF THE CORRESPONDENCE

yours to your brother my dear friend for some reason connected with your own deep family *clannishness* & the links between Llewelyn & me & between my brother Littleton & me hits me to the heart—for I tell you, I swear to you, I do **not** often come across this particular tone—*Our* family feeling our feeling to each other (as brothers who write)—though of *Theodore* Llewelyn & I have always been a bit over-awed not to say a tiny bit scared! But Llewelyn was never in the faintest degree scared of me nor I of him & we both would say the same of Littleton our Conservative! But your attitude to your brother my friend does really hit me mighty deep for I understand it O so well!

Yes sure I shall take advantage of your *Aristophanic aid* when the moment comes if it does that I want more books than I've got. Its a relief to my mind to have you in the background over Aristophanes to fall back upon at the sort of pinch *that may easily come.* But at *present* Ive got to just *narrow down on &* to the *text* with my 3 cribs. For like you—O how like our minds are!—its the actual *text* in its minute particulars as it sets off my frog-like soul on its hopping & croaking that's the chief thing.

Rather wildly & chaotically is just what I w^d and proudly too! boast of all my writings! We sure *are* most curiously alike my friend & *I am so glad you came.*

Yrs
J C Powys

II
Letters from Corwen
1950-April 1955

In the summer of 1950, after a hiatus in the correspondence of more than a year, G. Wilson Knight wrote to tell of the serious illness of his mother who had joined him at Leeds. Powys's response about his own gastric problems and solutions may make one clinical note appropriate; several critics—Knight among them—have discussed at some length Powys's concern with bodily functions, especially the enema administered to old Abel Twig by Sam Decker in A Glastonbury Romance *after his experience with the Grail and the 'gigantic spear . . . struck into his bowels.'*

Powys's unpublished letters confirm often that one result of his diet that excluded meat, fruits, and vegetables was dependence on enemas. In 1910 he first mentions using them, and in a letter of January 1932, to his sister Gertrude, written as he finished correcting page-proofs of A Glastonbury Romance, *he says: 'I have never had a natural action of the bowels since I went on this diet of milk and eggs,' a diet he seems to have maintained until his death in 1963, four months before his ninety-first birthday.*

After the death of Mrs Knight there is a four-year gap in the correspondence, broken after the publishers of Knight's study of Alexander Pope, Laureate of Peace, *sent Powys payment for permission to use a quotation. Knight dedicated* Laureate of Peace *to Powys with these words:*

LETTERS FROM CORWEN

To
John Cowper Powys
artist, teacher, seer
in
admiration

8

July 4th 1950.

My dear Friend

I'm proud of your having written to me at this serious moment with your mother so failing.

I'll tell you all about myself from this grim gastric view-point on the chance it may be of use. I've been always subject to gastric—I think duodenal—ulcers & have had 2 major operations one in my youth one in middle age but when after a haemorrhage I went to the Wrexham Emergency Hospital in the middle of this last war they'd given up operating for gastric trouble of my sort & they just put me on the operating table & used that *spying* process of putting a lamp down into your stomach which they call *'scop'*-something—no doubt from the Greek word for spying!

I came out better but suddenly got much worse & stayed worse for a couple of months or for three months till my *digestion refused everything* & I got to look like those ghastly concentration camp victims. At last I demanded of my doctor the presence of some terrific Specialist & he brought Dr Patterson the present Boss of the famous *Clinic* in Ruthin Castle. And he spent the aft examining and [asking] me questions. Then at the end he simply said: '*Try Olive Oil.*'

And this is what saved my life. I took it at once and day by day more and more—by itself—*pure olive-oil*, such as you can get fairly easily and such as in the war my American friends used to send me in rare quantities. And as I got stronger I could begin to take raw eggs & milk and tea again and finally was as well as I am today & I've been well *ever since*, for some three or four years or so!

Now I've given up all olive-oil; tho' I *like* it just as well, but I *didn't* want to depend on it. But it saved my life. It cured my complaint & saved me from dying of starvation!—caused solely by indigestion.

Now I walk up our mountain from 8.30 to 10.30 a m wet or fine. Then eat a quarter of a very very very stale & dry loaf munching it slowly though I can't eat much of the crust as for 10 years I've had no teeth, real or false! I'm so old a war horse of the Platform that having no teeth makes not the slightest difference to my speaking or reading—you wouldn't know I hadn't a tooth in my skull! But after my bread I swallow 2 raw eggs and follow them by 3, 4, 5, 6 cups of *very* strong tea with a *very* great deal of sugar in it! Then between noon and five I drink a bottle & a half of *Cold milk*. Then somewhere between five & six I have another quarter of a loaf—*half of a half loaf* of very stale bread (without butter or jam or treacle or honey or any of those things w^h I never touch. I *eat the dry bread dry*—like the old fashioned *prisoners*!—only *after it* I have all this strong sweet tea! and with this tea-time tea I only have one raw egg. So when I can get them, w^h of course isn't always! I have 3 eggs a day in addition to a bottle & a half of cold milk & tea twice a day with heaps of sugar!

But I was as near Death as indigestion could bring me. I couldn't digest a thimble-ful of milk! nor any of those children's foods—I was done for! If Pallas Athene herself—Κορη Διος αἰγιοχοιο γλαυκωπις Αθηνη ἀγελειη etc etc etc—had not saved my life with Olive Oil!

O my dear friend I do *so* follow your feelings at this juncture and I know something about it for my American Phyllis's aunt next door died on Phyllis's birthday (Nov 29) *last autumn* aged 86 & her mother now next door to us alone aged 84 is terribly shaky with all sorts of complaints & weaknesses and can walk *only with great difficulty* from room to room & never goes out—And both Phyllis & I know well this concentration of the *little things immediately around of* w^h *you speak.* I can not only follow it and understand it but practise it daily, **in preparation**!!

Yes I am already a pupil of yours in regard to different aspects of life & books & character which I've picked up from you so you will when I read you on Byron find me I mean your spirit between your pages will find me very amenable to your discoveries in Byron's nature. As to my long Romance of the Fifth Century entitled '*Porius,*' they made me shorten it by a *Third* which was *very* much against the grain! And even now they have not yet officially or finally accepted it but *I think they will*; but they talk of a *Limited Edition* & I dont like much *that idea.*

No I've had to postpone Aristophanes in order to

make sure of earning my living & since this delay about *Porius* I've been writing at top speed a penny dreadful pot-boiling Thriller about a Lunatic *Asylum*! [*The Inmates*]

The gods be with you my dear friend
Your affectionate and admiring
JOHN

Please call me John my friend & what may I call you? What does your Brother call you? What does 'G' stand for?

9

July 17 1950.

My dear **Richard**

for so I am in defiance of baptismal rites & of all restrictions bent on calling you, my friend—for my American Phyllis & I have had (& she's come to have 'got,' as we say, your 'number') long discussions as to why you have not as yet received your true recognition as a writer & interpreter of life & letters—and do you want, my friend, do you care, Richard, to hear our explanation? *We* hold that it's not Zodical or astrological *nor* regional-racial-national-traditional as I fancy is the cause of the grievous difficulty my *'Porius'* is having to get published which is very very largely due to the mysterious nature of Welsh words Welsh heroes & the profound Welsh *'élan de la Mort'*!! But purely numerolgical if there is such a word! Yes! we both hold very very strongly that the *drag* (for it's only a *delay* of course) in your arriving at your proper acceptance and recognition—is to be found in that accurst '**Wilson**!' Even if you'd been George Knight it would have been luckier but you **ought** to have been & you **really** *are* you know, *Richard Knight*. That they called you *Dick* in your secret family proves it for *they* knew you & *felt* instinctively this *secret occult numerological true destiny* interfered with so fatally by this un-natural 'Wilson.' Well! I wont go on but you know as I know the danger that lies in the mystery of *names*—good magic & bad magic both!

Well my dear Richard we know both of us right well the balm of Gilead it is to you to feel you nursed her to the end and saw it all through to an end in a manner worthy of the true mediterranean Hellenic Classical Tradition.

My **Phyllis** & I both do take *such peculiar interest* in all you did *over her cremation*—for Phyllis's mother's older sister whom she & Phyllis have looked after here for 15 years was cremated on the last day of last November.

We think very highly of that idea of yours of the *ashes in one spot*[1] that is an original idea *for Moderns*! in other words it is the *classical idea*—eh? and of that Beach Tree. It **was** decent of you Richard to take the trouble to help that Pittsburgh kid by telling him where to find those passages you mention in your own works.

Well, So Long! Of course I would most certainly & without scruple go to you for aid. But I'm of an optimistic turn of mind & I think my affairs will pick up.

Yrs as ever
John

Francis Berry & his Nancy & their child came to an Inn in Corwen for the night & we talked of you. I've known the surname Knight from childhood for my father's father married the *young widow* of a Mr Knight of Impington near Cambridge where he was a *don* & had to give up being a Don in consequence of marrying this pretty young *widow*.[2]

10

Aug 11 1950.

My dear *Richard*

Hurrah! O it does my heart good to hear of your great decision![3] Don't 'ee ever go back on it my dear friend or as our Welsh neighbours say—F'Annwyl Gyfaill for in 'cyfaill'—(friend)—the 'C' mutates—what the Welsh call *treigl* isn't that *some* word? 'treigl'!—into 'g' God knows why after 'F'annwyl' which only means 'my dear'!— is it a *treigl* or quivering tremblement of feeling? The spirits & the angeli & the demons alone know!

But I pray your brother has a happy time & a prosperous one in S. Africa. Our friend J. Redwood Anderson the Poet who has his lodging in Corwen is visiting S. Africa for 6 months starting in Nov but to see *his brother* more than anything else who has a *nursery garden* somewhere in that continent! You sure do have *piety* Richard in the true old classic sense, & I venerate you for it.

Yrs ever
John

Not a proper letter only an acknowledgment and *not* to be re-acknowledged by *thee*!

I I

May 19th 1954.

My dear Professor

I do indeed thank you ever so for this extra Guinea forwarded faithfully by Mr Greenwood of the Bodley Head—a guinea for love as you might say! O but, my dear friend, I am so thankful that you are writing a book on Pope.

I have been so often of late saying to my old American Friend Miss Playter to whom Llewelyn dedicated his 'Love & Death' that its simply mad that among our modern re-appraisals of old Masters no really good book has been more than 'dedicated' to Pope has been holding him up & turning him round & diving into his soul! Aye! but he *was* a genius & a *great* little man ... & I tell you my dear Professor I simply rejoice that its you—you *'your wone self'* and *none other* who is now 'dedicating'—I don't know for what queer occult reason that particular word keeps rushing into the top of my pen-nib!—*yourself* to this demanded this needed but this by *no means* easy task of painting a real perfect oil-colour Portrait of Alexander Pope!

Well, the gods be with you my friend, and may the Muses not only *support* you but inspire you as you proceed in this rare task. You certainly have the luck-bearing benediction of this old Druidic—'ribbon-development'

tho' it may be—hearthstone—'your Phowys'
Yrs ever
J C Powys

12

Monday May 24 1954.

My dear *dear* friend

I do thank you 100000 times for DEDICATING your Book on Pope to me. I am thrilled to think of it.

I swear to you, my friend, that as a literary person you are as a writer of subtle insight and imagination you are as a penetrating critic you are exactly *'after my heart,'* as we have come to say, tho' its an odd expression with 'after' in the sense of according to the reverence & admiration and affection I have for you—reverence towards you, admiration of you and affection for you! But I shall be proud of this dedication. I am very easily made to feel such exuberant pride & vanity and both these things (usually reprobated) I encourage in myself for I go without the faintest effort whenever I think my conscience orders it to the other extreme when I think of myself as a weak loquacious fussy comical and in many things very *very* stupid—fool! No no—**conceit** is the unpleasant thing both for him who is conceited and for his relations especially his wife!! and next especially his *sisters*! His brothers & his Dad don't bother about his bloody conceit in fact they are secretly rather pleased to feel superior to such a fucking ass! And his mother is ready to *encourage it*—for in *her* heart she so greatly adores him that she feels it to be quite proper that he should also think highly of himself—for he *is* wonderful—and *She bore this wonder! She bore Him!*

O but my dear friend I do seriously think—no! no! don't smile with the thought that I'm flattering. I *am* a very devil of a flatterer I mean I *can* be & *easily* be; but I *never* flatter my real friends. No it is serious when I say that the gods have given you the divinest & in many ways the luckiest *and* happiest of all their gifts—*Humility*. You do in this *without question* beat all the rest of us writing experts and I can tell you that of all the virtues (except the sort of *Metaphysical pride* of *Nietzsche* and *poetical pride* of *Dante*) and that profound humour of Rabelais of w^h you speak & (O I be proud of praising it!) and I would add the humour of Sterne for in the subtlest and deepest humour (while it so beautifully *fools* its *opposite* like Shakespeare with Falstaff & Dickens with so many!) there must I seem to fancy be a self-humility that if we went to the bottom of we'd go go down that deep crack in the bottom of the ocean floor of this little planet that leads a bit further than to the Antipodes.

You **must** pay us a visit my dear friend one day—for my companion of over 30 years now who lives with me here in Corwen as 'Mrs Powys' but really is *Miss Phyllis Playter* an American Citizen from the *Middle West* born in *Kansas City Missouri & educated in Boston*! was out when you came and has only her old Boswellian mate Jack Johnny John's description of you to know how nice you are *and she's dying to see you*—so do I beg you my dear friend one of these days ere this Summer's over get into your head that you ought to see Snowdon again & look in on us on your way there or back. I shall be soon reading with *concentrated excitement both these* booklets you have given me, you can be sure.

Yrs as ever
J C Powys

You speak so nicely of Theodore that I *must* tell you that my only child[4] died on the Yes on the Sixteenth of February this year and is buried in Bath where his mother lies who died about 6 years ago. He was a Roman Catholic Priest and his Will was a Rabelaisian one for he left a pound a head to those who came to his *Wake* & there were 100 priests there!

13

May the 29th 1954.

Mr dear Friend I **have** just to tell you how thrilled I am by this article of yours on M. Murry's *SWIFT!*[5] It is a pity that Murry can't follow your Dostoievskyan suggestion & go *a bit* mad when he interprets madness!

For O! how I do agree with you here—And how wise & right you are to insist that none of us have yet discovered (& that very very likely no critic will *ever fathom* to the bottom) this strange *'malaise'* as you so well put it 'which proves more vital than health'—

Aye! but I do so rejoice in reading these words of yours: 'though whether *Sanity* is the last word in wisdom in expounding the significance of the Insane—may be questioned—

Well! it *will* be wonderful if fate eventually does

allow us to have a call from you either in your goings out or comings in—

Yrs as ever
John

14

November 16 1954.

My dear Dick

Yes for the sake of all the gods lets be Dick & Jack to each other for its Jack rather than John I am to what are left of the Ten brothers & sisters I used to have— 5 brothers & 5 sisters—tho' my oldest surviving one (for your John-Jack-Johnny was the first-born) always calls me *Johnny*; for we were infants together in Shirley Vicarage Derbyshire—*Derbyshire born Derbyshire bred ... Strong in the arm & weak in the head.* We were as infants 'Johnny and Littleton' and thro' his greater physical prowess in the fields of cricket and football and his general *authority* having become very very soon Head of the Prep at Sherborne has from School Days when he was always *a form above me* and always better at the classics when confronted with writing *Greek Verse* in the Fourth Form & 'did a bunk' into *chemistry* where I told myself stories of being a sort of Dorsetshire Faust and thats why very likely Ive turned to Roger Bacon and am now trying to compose a Metaphysical-Magician's tale [*The Brazen Head*] about the last years of the nephew of Ivanhoe's *Cour-de-Lion*! Poor old Henry III— I have only now very now discovered *how long* that

D

poor shaky monarch survived as king! Roger B. was ruined (with his brother & uncle) for taking this King's side in the civil war against the Simon de Montfort—the side I w^d certainly have taken for I hate Simon de Montfort & all those Bloody Barons! And isnt it funny my friend that nowadays we make such a hell of a fuss about *Magna Charta* when it wasn't *'the People'* but a set of rascals far crueller & more barbarous than ever King John was who won that famous Runnymede Victory! God! my friend *you* or someone with your peculiar gifts ought to write a book called The Popular Clichés of History or you might say directly 'The **Lies** of History' *as she has been taught* for a thousand odd years! I tell you I have been simply shocked by reading about the Manorial System—*It turns a person into an urbanite!* for it looks *to me* as if in those Ages the *Towns* & *Cities* were the only originators and sanctuaries of personal and individual liberty! Build the walls of Jerusalem and Athens! as against these thrice damnable country Manors! I can tell you my friend Ive learnt more history from writing romantic stories than I ever learnt at school.

 O my *dear friend* but I'm so thrilled and proud that you quoted my Rabelais book towards the end. But apart from the *eternal Me* business w^h must be the cause why all writers today hide away from each other & are so scared of each other. Putting yourself aside the only writers I'm not far too funky of to write freely to are Henry Miller of *Big Sur California*. There's an address for you, aye? James Hanley who brought *us* here [to Corwen]—*'us'*—now that my only offspring who was a born huntsman and poet and died at 51 a Roman his children for walks about a Giant & a Fairy and the fact that I had to cajole & clownerize and ensorcerize ten younger brothers and sisters in my youth (*not all my life* for I've outlived all but 2 brothers and 3 sisters!)—into my own favourite world of gods and monsters that made me into a Myth-Maker!

Your grateful
Jack

[*Four postscripts around the margins*]
And O I do pray that one day you'll cross our threshold again!
We shant be moving to Blaenau, Ffestiniog till New Year.
O I am more and more & more pleased because my name is associated with your Pope and I love to think that yours (Wilson & all!) will be associated with his name forever! but of course since my god-mother's father's name was Knight and only after he was dead her mother married my grandfather Ive been brought up to respect that name from childhood [. It is] because I found 'Tommy Wilson' one of our Masters at school a trial to me personally tho' he was a great Cricketer that I've got this crazy Wilsonian *Tich*!
A scrawl of *thanks only* & *not* to be *acknowledged*

Yr old Jack o'Lantern or Jack out of the Box or Jack & the Bean *Stalk*!

[*On envelope*]
O by the way just see if it isn't 'gulfs' not 'deeps' that 'wash us down' in Tennyson's Ulysses.

JOHN COWPER POWYS TO WILSON KNIGHT

16

Tuesday the Fifth of April 1955.

My dear Friend

I think we shall be *still here* in this same house on the 15th (Friday)

So if you came from Exeter via Bristol and Shrewsbury you would change for Corwen at *Ruabon* where you can get a train or a bus *via Llangollen* and we could book a room for the night for you at the *Owen Glyndwr* Hotel in Corwen if you wrote to say you would arrive that evening on Friday 15th.

Then you could walk up the hill from the hotel and see us that night or if you felt too weary for that after such a long journey you could come up *next morning* on the *16th Saturday* and leave Corwen by the noon *12 o'clock train* going to Ruabon *via Llangollen*.

I expect you would have to *change at Shrewsbury* for *Stoke upon Trent* in the *Five Towns*—and I expect if you left Corwen at 12 o'clock noon and changed at Ruabon you would be able to get a good train from *Shrewsbury* to the *Five Towns* possibly *via* Stafford but anyway from Shrewsbury there must be trains in plenty going to *Stoke* and *Newcastle-under-Lyme* and the other two towns in that Pottery district *sacred to the memory of Arnold Bennett!*

It will be wonderful to see you again and *this* time you'll see my Phyllis—but I fear *not* our new home, which is the *hell of a place to reach by train*—one of the reasons why we are going there.

yrs ever

J.C. Powys

If you came up to see us after going to your room in the Owen Glyndwr the night of the 15th you *could* leave if you wanted to by a good train to Ruabon at *9 a m* in the *morning*!

P.S. There are no Sunday trains into or out of Corwen!

17

Monday April 25 [1955].
my brother Littleton's
82nd birthday—I think![8]

If so we shall both be 82 till next October when I'll be 83! But I *may* be wrong—He *may* only be or he only may be 81! I must ask him to tell me. Its cruel how his legs have failed him with this thrice accurst arthritis. But he gets great thrills from being driven over all that West Country so familiar to us from our school-days!

You were so nice my dear friend to write to Phyllis like you did—but you can bet I've already read every word of this thrilling & most exciting essay on the Scholar Gipsy.[9] God! my friend but I can tell you I got the shock of exquisite glory when I came suddenly among these great Shades bolt on my own name! But you *are* wonderful at these things—simply wonderful. And O how true is your word that we do want *fresh new Insights suddenly thrown* upon these Ancient Favourites of ours.

O I should say so!

How that 'undid their corded bales' is echoed & echoed by one milestone after another in the widening hill & dale land & sea pilgrimage of my manias for certain *favourite* books & poems! And what grand *daring* of yours—you *are* the *sort* of Guide we *need* indeed!— to make the **Tyrian** the hero of this *as against* the stealthy light-hearted merry ones!! O there is something that hugely excites & disturbs me there! & its *Nietzschean* in *the best sense*!

I'll never forget—& I bet I share this with lots of *others* both old & young!—the *startling piercing* illuminated look in your eyes as *you spoke of this & of that—* **But** *Beware* of the Occult! my dear friend O *beware of it*! You and I have enough of the Demonic in us *without that*! its *effect on us* is a weakening one & a blurring one and *not* an enlightening one. Beware! Beware! Beware O maestro mine!

your old John

We *may* go off before this week ends or at the beginning of next week but for the next four or five days *anyway* here we bide still—confound it!

III
Letters from Blaenau Ffestiniog
May 1955-February 1957

At last came the move to Blaenau Ffestiniog in the slate-producing hills ten miles southwest of Mt Snowdon where John Cowper Powys lived his remaining years, writing constantly. Indeed, it seems doubtful that any author has had so productive a ninth decade—ten publications, one major book a year, all but Lucifer, *the 120-page blank verse epic of 1905, written or completed between 1951 and 1960.*

Twenty-five years younger and fully engaged in the classroom and in the theatre at Leeds, G. Wilson Knight was equally energetic; his bibliography for this period lists fifteen articles and six books, including the 'Byron Book' discussed in the following letters: Lord Byron's Marriage, The Evidence of Asterisks.

Although Powys's letters to others confirm that he kept well posted on contemporary events, these letters carry two rare mentions to 'the Professor' on worldly matters: during the Suez crisis he speaks of Nasser and the petrol shortage. The letters show also an instance of the forgetfulness of which Powys sometimes complained. He tells here of practicing sadism 'once in my whole life,' but his Autobiography *of 1934 suggests two more: 'I only practised sadism about three times in all my days; on those worms in the Northwold Summer-House, on those newly-hatched little birds in the Sherborne quarry,—*

and even of that *incident I am doubtful—and on those beetles I once killed at Rothesay House with scalding water. Never has any cerebral vice been as exacting, as exclusive, as limited in its scope, as mine.*'

18

1 Waterloo, Blaenau-Ffestiniog, Merionethshire.
May 12 1955.

Not a letter my dear friend only to say I am greatly relieved to hear that I needn't be scared on your behalf over 'thik little job' of the Occult!

Yes in return I'll obey thee *to the letter*—in fact I am having a *letter printed* to tell all my friends that I am going to do nothing but write books till I die *holding my pen*.[1]

Yes we both simply worship this little house and this amazing City in the Clouds but O it takes time arranging furniture in Dolls' Houses!!

Yr ever grateful
John

19

Thursday Sept 26 1956.

My dear Friend

I am simply thrilled by your wonderful *Review* of Lucifer. Aye! but you *do me proud*! And it was a lovely present to have from you your own brother's Virgil.[2]

Aye! my friend but how clearly I remember the piercing & almost hypnotic look you have in your eyes! Your influence upon your disciples must be Hippocratic! A ruler you are I bet my life over the wildest young horses!

Simultaneously with 'The Brazen Head' Macdonald's are soon publishing my brother Littleton's book—he died of a fall in his study near Glastonbury—entitled '*Still the Joy of it*' in which he talks freely of all his Ten brothers & sisters & praises his second wife the writer Elizabeth Myres [Myers] who wrote 'The Basilisk of St James's' & 'The Well full of Leaves.' He & I were together as 'Johnny & Littleton' in the Nursery, in the Prep, at School, and at Coll.

Now I've only got one brother left W. E. Powys of Kenya and three sisters— So we are only 5 who used to be eleven!

Yes Miss Playter & I *both* like Blaenau *more* & *more*!

Your ever loyal
J C Powys

[*On envelope*]
Please thank your Brother a great deal from me for this V—*especially* since the Book has his *Signature*

20

Wednesday Dec 5 1956.

Mr dear Friend

Aye! but I did so appreciate your article in the

Twentieth Century [on *Lucifer*]. I can *now* see & always do when I write to you or read you or hear of you or think of you—your **penetrating** *eyes*! I bet you're the only Professor in Europe with such eyes! They are rare in all professions; but in poetry & literature almost extinct. Dante may have had eyes like yours but I bet Plato's were cloudy with subjective mists and Aristotle's were probably like old Prof Seeley's whom I used to hear lecturing when I was an undergrad & who lectured from his chair on the platform, thoughtful & concentrated, as if contemplating mathematical equations written in Space!

But I was indeed mighty proud & happy I can tell you over all your words in this article & I got down the book at once & corrected those two mistakes.[3]

I forbid you my friend to acknowledge the receipt of this scrawl by anything *but your blessing thro' this misty air* which will buck me up in what I'm doing now which will take me the unknown alone knows how long— a sort of thought-reading paraphrase & psychological running reverberation of—the *Iliad*!! [*Homer and the Aether*] I was so pleased to have your brother's *Aeneid*.

Yours always & ever and may Jehovah do for Nasser!

J C Powys

With respects from Miss P. Playter.

21

Tuesday night Dec 11th 1956.
Aye! my dear Professor I am indeed thrilled to think

that there *may* appear something of thine in the Yorkshire Post on all Three Books Lucifer[,] Brazen Head & Still the Joy of it by Littleton.

No no! you never sent this Picture of yourself as Timon. I am thrilled by it. Well! my dear friend you beat me who am also a born actor but I suspect more still of a born Circus clown and lets hope *at my best* a born (Shakespearean or not) **Stage Clown**!

But you've beaten me hollow in this picture of yourself as Timon. Aye! but I am thrilled to have it. Where you beat me is *baring your shoulders*!

I couldn't bring myself to do that—all my sedentary book-worm love of warmth, all my shyness and shrinking from being seen in my lean funny-looking nakedness— no *shyness isnt* the word. What can it be? What can it be? But I should refuse even if the Queen herself ordered me to undress and bare my shoulders! However hot the weather and burning the sun I *couldn't* do it! And I *know* I should have felt the same as a boy and as an undergraduate! What is it. Sexually I am a Voyeur and a Sadist. Some say a bit of a Masochist too— But I fancy *all* Sadists have a touch of Masochism! They go together! but no touch of Masochism would make me bare my shoulders! But I do greatly love this picture of you as Timon.

All good luck to you my dear friend from us both
ever your old grateful
J C Powys

22

Sunday January the 6th 1957.

My dear Friend

O I am so pleased with this your article kept anonymous by the Paper but now revealed privately as between friends to be thine own writing upon Littleton's 'Still the Joy of It.' It is exciting to think that you've been writing for The Yorkshire Post a review of L C P's *Still the Joy* and Redwood Anderson's *Almanac [and Other Poems]* and my Brazen Head *all together*. Yes as old Littleton says he owed to Elizabeth Myers his friendship with a *whole group* of very interesting and spirited young ladies who were passionate devotees of her & who when she died came constantly to visit him— One of them sat up by his coffin almost all night in Sherborne Abbey before he was buried there by the side of his first wife Mabel.

I really think I may boast to have a lot in common with you as far as this *acting* tendency goes but I never had the privilege of dressing up for any favourite part so as to feel that **I was 'It'** or the imaginary 'He' as you have clearly done from this picture of Timon. But there's no doubt that the two strongest tendencies in my life are a craving to invent fairy-tales or hero-tales or crime-tales and mystery-tales and a craving to recite them on a stage or a *platform* and I have always shunned the stage— Why? I can tell you *exactly* why! Because I've got a mania against *seeing* myself! I look hastily away if there's any risk of a glimpse of myself in any mirror!

I worship all my *sensations* chiefly the sensation

of *warmth* second of drinking just the right kind of Milk and of swallowing just the right kind of dry stale bread, white bread! Since I turned 80 I have lost *all* sexual excitement. Though I rather fancy its Kant's mysterious Categorical Imperative outside Space and Time or to put it simply Conscience that prevents my reading the sadistic books that I used to bring back from Paris—in *English* they were! So I can't be the only British Sadist who depends on Paris for his special literature! Heaven, or perhaps Hell alone knows how I managed to beget my beautiful beloved son a Roman Catholic Priest and now buried aged 51 in Bath. There was never the faintest filial or paternal relation between us: we were simply devoted friends who *knew everything* just *everything* about each other's sexual peculiarities— We were like an elderly orator of the heathen days with some youth between whom there was not the faintest homo-sexual love but just deep and understanding *comradeship*.

Yes, I've never known what is called the *passion of love* but I have *always* known romantic poetical idealised love.

My sex feeling my erotic feeling my lecherous feeling is entirely[4]   and has been so since I was a little boy and asked my mother what chastity meant and she replied the opposite of what you do—meaning masturbation. For I've always been a terrible masturbator and if I had any grandchildren w^h of course is impossible as my son was a priest of the Roman church I should unhesitatingly advise them to masturbate! But, as I say, since turning 80 I have lost all temptation in *that* direction & never give it a thought; though my *romantic ideal-*

ization still goes on, almost as strong as ever, and *will* go on till I die!

By the way do tell me my dear friend **When** is *'Twelfth Night'* and what does it celebrate? And what does it exactly mean? And when did it start?

Oh yes! and in the Spring as you suggest in March or April it'll be lovely to see you again and have a good talk with you. And my Phyllis Player still an American Citizen *says the same.*

Yrs with real gratitude, the gratitude of the eldest of a family who all have as our best friend Louis Umfraville [Umfreville] Wilkinson says a certain *barbaric naiveté*!.

John Cowper Powys

23

SADISM was the missing word!

Monday Jan. 14 1957.

My dear Friend

I do indeed most deeply thank you for your wonderful & most Comprehensive Summary of Twelfth Night. I loved all those Wassail songs and the whole thing is Completely new knowledge to me. What a man you are for real Historic knowledge & the power of making it exciting! — — — I am longing for the Byron Book. What lucky lucky kids—or lucky young devils!—your pupils must be!

Well! Miss P & I pray the Petrol will last well into Spring & I shall once more sway this way & that way under your piercing glances!

O I did so well like your article on *Spiritualism*. I won't say 'you hit the nail on the head' for there aint no nail nor no head but I *will* say you caught *that cloud* the shape of a magician's hand as it crossed the wavy line between the end of the horizon and the beyond the end of the horizon!

I shall surely treasure both your Twelfth *Night* shock of precious stalks and your words about those tap tap tap What is that knocking? atmospheric procession? *They come* graymalkin Paddock calls! fair is foul & foul is fair! hover through the fog and filthy air!

Goethe's word about Byron showed how strong his attraction to Byron was—& *just because* 'when he thinks he is a child'—I hope I'll get thro' my present Homeric studies quickly enough to write something in praise of *Second childhood* for if *theirs* is the kingdom of heaven what about doubling 'theirs' with the dotage of a *second go* at that 'something far more deeply interfused'?

ever gratefully
yr old
J C Powys

24

Friday Jan 18 1957.

My dear Friend

I have already read the whole of your last chapter of the Byron Book and I am most impressed and a bit staggered by all you have discovered. Think of Byron having homosexual tendencies! It was ever so good of you to give the book to me. It is all of it completely new ground to my old-fashioned head & still older-fashioned pitch-fork and spade! I had never even *heard* of the *Leon* poems far less read them, and the idea of Byron's being addicted to homosexual practises is absolutely new to me! Am I right in assuming that you prove here that his lady was as much of a Lesbian as he was a Sodomite and she had a passionate Lesbian love for Augusta and her anger and vengeance were stirred up more by jealousy than anything else and that jealousy was at the bottom— no bad word in regard to this queer group!—of the campaign of vengeance she entered upon against him—and does your exciting discovery extend so far as the discovery that Byron used to embrace his wife 'per anum' *rather than the other way round,* having an 'anal complex'? Did Byron write those Leon poems or *were they written by George Colman?* Being completely ignorant of those Leon Poems I find *this* a rather puzzling point.

On page 114 I see that you say 'Before talking to Mrs Stow Lady B. had been spreading among her friends the scandal of both incest *and another crime.*' I find it a little puzzling and difficult to follow clearly.

If I knew a little more about the other characters in this queer drama such as Lovelace and Hobhouse I might be able to follow it all more clearly. It sure *is* an exciting book and I do thank you awfully for it.

Yrs gratefully
J. C. Powys

As for my own Sadism which has always been until all sex desire left me some five or six years ago my only erotic urge—I only practised it *once* in my whole life and that was upon a lot—Oh! a great lot—of *earth-worms* that in an arbour in my grandfather's garden when I was still at school and about 17 I cut with a knife into innumerable bits and threw into a fountain—when everybody was at church and I was safe from interruption.

25

Wednesday, Jan. 23, 1957.
My dear Friend & Master in Discernment

I do thank you not only for the Byron Book but for your wise & clear answer to my questions. Yes Phyllis & I get the *Sunday Times* so we saw that excellent article on your book & I do heartily congratulate you on it—I bet it will arouse a great deal of interest.

Many of my best early friends were Homos & O I tried very very hard to become one myself! But all to no purpose! I never in my life felt the faintest tendency in that direction. But the odd thing about my eroticism is that I've always been terrified of *'having'* a girl—It was a kind of miracle that I managed to beget my son. But oh! How thankful I was and am & ever shall be that I did for he was about the best friend I've ever had! We understood each other through & through & never concealed anything from each other. We knew each other in & out & through & through! And it wasn't 'Paternal & Filial' at all—never from the start! It was like those friendships between an older & younger man which are so powerful but in which the bond is *pure affection* with nothing homosexual about it.

Yes my sex-life has been from start to finish 'cerebral' as they call it in other words life-long masturbation till I was 80 when *all suddenly sex desire ended entirely!* No I have not had the faintest stirring of my Prick since I was 80! But now a very interesting thing is that while my greatest sex pleasure was in reading certain sadistic books that I used to buy in *Paris in English*—I could not find them *anywhere else*—No not even in *Brussels*! If I tried to read—to read one of those books *now*—it would be *against my conscience*! Think of *conscience outlasting desire*!! For I can recall the exact spot on the Dorset coast near Lulworth where I decided that I could not *even from fear of Hell* give up my *cerebral orgies of sadism*! I remember that I *was afraid* of going to Hell but no! my cerebralistic vice was too strong!

Well good luck my friend and may there be enough oil *off* the troubled waters for our little Spring colloquy.

Yrs ever
J C Powys & Miss Playter
sends her best too

I do think that *perhaps* some of my masochism that **may** (I am *not* sure about this!) *accompany sadism* **still** often activates my conduct but of course I tend to regard it as Christian *virtue*!!

26

Woden's Day Feb 6 1957.

O I hope you & your friend *will* manage to reach

us. I tell you my best of all Professors that the comfort & consolation & help you w^d be to thousands & thousands of youths of my sort—I can't answer for young women tho' I profoundly suspect 'twould be the same with them—if you could go about thro' the whole of our Island as a new kind of *Missionary*—a missionary showing young people—just the *opposite* of christian teaching—*not* how to suppress sex but how to get the greatest amount of thrilling pleasure out of it—and I believe a lot of your teaching would be an *encouragement* to masturbation. In fact teaching the young how to get the greatest thrills out of masturbation—you see we used to be told & my life has proved it just *simply a lie* that it was very bad you [for?] you to masturbate— that it did you great harm—I **know** that *that* is a lie. It does you great good & not only *you* for I bet Jack the Ripper would never have become a criminal if he had been taught how to enjoy his ripping *in imagination* while he masturbated with the sensation of it. He would not have ripped anybody then!

 I tell you the purest chastest girl I ever knew was a friend of mine called Lily whom my wife—there's a noble spirit *and so she was*—allowed me to have as a guest & visitor in our house—and she was a regular prostitute and I recall well how she used to pad her little bottom with leather pads to make it more appealing! She *vanished* in the end like DeQuincey's tart who saved his life by spending her earnings on buying him expensive wine.

 O my dear Professor the good you could do if you were to go through all our land advocating Masturbation—

I dare say for both sexes—but I cannot speak for young ladies—as a cure for all ills! In other words telling sex-maniacs to *use their imagination on themselves* and **not** on **others**! I bet if Gilles de Retz had been ready to learn from me from Jack the Imaginary Ripper his 250 victims would have *descendants still alive*! But notice the proof that the *wisest* people in the world are children I must not add old rogues in their *second childhood!* and what are the wisest books in the world Not the Bible or the Koran or the Vedanta but *Grimms Fairy Tales* & *Mother Goose Tales including Blue Beard* in their scope. Jesus was right there. We grown ups have no idea of what children see and know & live by & *suffer* too sometimes just as Jesus did! Well I am your old

                      Jawing John C. Powys

P.S. Hurrah for your **Book** on *Drama*!

27

February 27 Wednesday 1957.

Hurrah! my dear Professor! I'm certainly thrilled to think that Phyllis and your old John are actually to have a visit from you and your friend Oliver Campion I bet he is of the same blood as the Poet of that name. I wish I had some of the *real blood* of Cowper to match with his Campion blood! We both carefully note the precise time & date of your Knock at the *Door of Our House!*—Waterloo 1 & 2—*Ours* is 1—for Waterloo is only the name of a House *not* of a *street*—*One House divided into two*! and *ours* is *Number One*! There is a Café two minutes away on *the main Blaenau Road* called the *Dom Café* and our house is **up** *a little slope East of this Don Café.*[5]

We note that you will get *fairly near* to us on Monday April 1st *All Fool's Day* which I shall celebrate as I always do with a full heart, for I am a born Alderman in *that* little Corporation, but with an extra expectation of the Morrow!. And then on April 2nd *we'll expect you in the afternoon.*

Yes Phyllis and I noticed with pleasure how the Newspapers were talking of your Byron Book. *You are indeed* my dear Professor coming into your own! I rejoice in your suggestion that certain Monastic Orders have secretly to their own fresh Initiates advocated cerebral masturbation as the greatest of all possible devices for keeping our vices to ourselves! When I've finished—if I live to do so—my Iliad book—I'd love to write a book entitled *Second Childhood* wherein I shall show the weird strange curious mysterious magnetic psychic *understanding* that exists between *really* old people such as I am now—*much older* than I was when I wrote *'The Art of Growing Old'*—and Babies and Toddlers and *all children* up to 4!! It is a most interesting thing. A week ago I went to see a Doctor about a Touch of *Fibrositis*—no! (I forget everything in this dotage I'm [I?] want to analyze in my book!) it was about a *scratch* I had in my dead blind eye—and in the Surgery waiting room we were about a dozen *adults* or even 15 and one tiny child of about 2. *It* and *I* sat gravely in the circle. Then very gravely I waved to it. And with equal gravity it waved back at me. It was just as if we had both said to each other: 'Lord! what fools these grown up mortals be!'

O I pray and *shall* pray really and truly to Jehovah & to Athene too that April 2 bring you both.

Yrs ever
J C Powys

IV
Letters from Blaenau Ffestiniog
May 1957-December 1957

Although the correspondence of Powys and Knight covers twenty-five years, more than one-third of John Cowper Powys's fifty letters were written in 1957. Accumulated years did not slow him, nor the task of continuing to earn his living with his pen. Finances were a problem throughout his life, for, after relatively good sales of his works in the early 1930s, no one of his later books was a commercial success. He had no pension, and the modest inheritance from his father a third of a century earlier had long since gone.

And yet it seems certain that even with financial security his love of inventing tales and his 'craving to recite them' would have kept him at his daily writing adventure. During the period covered by the following letters, Powys read page-proofs of the recently completed Up and Out *(published in August 1957), wrote an introduction to his brother Llewelyn's* Somerset and Dorset Essays, *and continued writing* Homer and the Aether. *In July 1957, he sprang to the defence of American novelist James Purdy in a letter to* The Observer. *And he kept up his voluminous correspondence[1] with many people—his way, perhaps, quite isolated in North Wales, of conversing and reciting in his eighty-fifth year.*

Knight's review of Up and Out *in the* Times Literary Supplement *of October 1957, praised so highly by*

JOHN COWPER POWYS TO WILSON KNIGHT

Powys in these letters as the 'perfect analysis' of his 'nature and work and life,' is reprinted in Appendix 1. Knight's 'Drama Book,' encouraged here by Powys, appeared in 1962 as The Golden Labyrinth: A Study of British Drama.

28

Thursday May 23 1957.

My dear Friend

O it was wonderful to see your hand on the envelope! Think of your going to Munich the first week in June & going to lecture there on *Shakespeare's Kings*. God! What a thrilling subject! I keep your Timon of Athens picture which I do value so in my Welsh Dictionary so that I see it saying to me *'I hate Mankind*!!!' when I begin— probably under the influence of all these Sheep & Lambs who walk up and down so complacently here as if they owned the Town *which as a literal legal fact* they do or their farmers do! For the quarry people only got the quarries for their special purposes and all the real landowners are farmers, I am toning down my prejudices! But Oh My dear friend! Do for the sake of Math the son of Mathonwy, and of Rhiannon whose child Dylan, when they took it to the sea to baptyze it swam off and was no more seen, get hold of Lady Charlotte Guest's *'Mabinogion'* which was published in the *'Everyman'* Series! None of these modern translators *touch* Lady Charlotte Guest and her *notes* are full of just that rich dark mysterious suggestiveness that a real scholar like you can appreciate best.

My own favourite of all my stories is **Atlantis** wherein I pretend that Odysseus *discovers America* after having visited Atlantis!

Phyllis tells me that Lady Charlotte Guests version of the Mabinogion is *out of Print now*. But you *might* come across it in some 2^d hand book-shop. But what she suggests for me to do is very sound & good & I'll soon do it & that is to send you a copy of *the new Mabinogion* by Professor Glyn Jones of Aberystwyth College with whom I have stayed ere now & who has been very kind to me. In fact he brought a Professor from *Iceland* to visit us in Corwen which delighted me as when I was a boy 'Theodolph (or *Theooderic*) The Icelander' was my favourite book! A book by *La Motte Fouqué author of Undine*. So I'll send you as a present— because I owe so much to you my friend—this new Mabinogion by Prof Glyn Jones & another Aberystwyth Professor. I daresay its *a lot more up to date in its scholarship* than my adored Lady Charlotte's version! But after *Atlantis* (and *it* is also published by Macdonald) my favourite story & this brings in the *Mithras* cult in Wales & also *King Arthur* and *Also Merlin* is a book called *Porius* and this introduces *'The Porius Stone'* which is in The National Museum of Wales in *Cardiff* and a **replica** of it is still in the wild hills near here they tell me! This *Porius* tale is in the year A D 400 or *round about* then; and begins with *'The Gaer'* a great Maiden Castle-like prehistoric Fortress above Corwen.

All good luck to your Munich experience.

yrs ever
J C Powys

JOHN COWPER POWYS TO WILSON KNIGHT

[*On envelope*]
How *very* good of you to write that script for Raymond Garlick who is such a good friend of us here.²

29

Saturday June 29 1957.

My dear Professor

I am so proud to be associated in any way with this wonderful pupil of yours young Mr Alan Sommers & his B.Litt at Oxford.³ O I am so glad that you my dear friend are going to write a Book on English Drama. You know the odd thing is that Welsh has changed very little. A. Sommers wont find anything like the great difference between Mediaeval Welsh and modern Welsh as between, say, Chaucer and Tennyson! Lady Charlotte has shown this to us. I am especially glad you like Jobber Skald⁴ because it has just been translated by a French lady a friend of ours who has been here with her sister (who is an astronomer!) and she has another sister who is a good novelist and a painter. These three young ladies have no parents but live together at Port Royal Paris. Their father like Napoleon came from Corsica. It is to be published shortly but I don't know the date by *Plon*, under the title of *'Les sables de la Mer.'*

O yes my dear friend we shall be delighted to see Mr Sommers as time goes on, a bit later in the year, for just now we seem so overpowered by letters and visitors that for the last few days Ive been unable to do any work at all! O yes I used to have essays to correct when

I was an Extension Lecturer for Cambridge Oxford & London before I escaped to America & earned my living there for 30 odd years & brought back my Miss Playter *who is still a USA Citizen*. I was so delighted to see in U.S. Consulate in Liverpool a noble picture of *Nathaniel Hawthorne*.

How annoying that the Times Lit Sup should behave like that. Its wrong of them. I cant understand it. And don't I know the weariness & tiresomeness of *marking essays* & placing them in order! I escaped from that when I went to America. Its a shame your trip to Germany had to be so brief. Now do let me come to an exciting personal matter. My godmother who was my Aunt Philippa, my Father's half-sister, married a learned Oxford Don of Christ Church called Shirley and had two sons and three daughters of whom my Cousin *Ralph* and my Cousin *Alice* were my inspirers in Literature when I was young. Cousin Alice took me to see Frau Foster Nietzsche just after *his death* & I had the run of his library—all French books!—while the ladies talked while Cousin Ralph introduced me to W.B. Yeats with whose Father & sister I crossed to America.

But when my Father's Father who was Bursar of Corpus Cambridge fell in love with my grandmother she was then the widow (with little Philippa as a child) of a *Mr Knight* whose home was Impington Hall within a walk of Cambridge. I have often wondered whether this father of my god-mother was by some queer chance a relative of yours?

Well I must obey my one eye which says: 'Ill go on strike if you don't go to bed!' and stop. But O my friend

I do think these lads are lucky to have you as their guide.

 Yrs, 'while this machine is to him,'
    J C Powys & so
    says my Phyllis.

30

[Postmarked: 9 Jly 57]

[*Postcard*]

 O I am so thrilled my dear friend to hear that when my *'Up and Out'* a right crazy tale of time & eternity & the Other side of the Moon! comes out you'll be writing on *'little me,'* as the girls *don't* say! at free length in the Times Lit. Sup. Talk of kindness & consideration it isnt often that a learned gent like thou art takes the cake at thik little job!

31

September 30 1957.

 You can bet your life, Professor dear, that both your old Johannis & his Miss Playter are looking forward eagerly to this Lit-Sup. It'll be a Parnassian 'sup' & an Heliconian 'Sip' and I sure *will indeed, when I get it,* tell you all. I don't think we get the Times Lit Sup any more—though we get the Times itself & the Telegraph every day—so for the sake of all the Olympians please send it or get it sent to us! I *sure will* study it carefully and let you know exactly *where*—but I doubt it'll be *anywhere*—we disagree. I hope my most penetrating of all Professors you don't feel it too much of an effort after your rest in Exeter to start your College work again.

Well! The next time I'll write will be to tell you my reactions to your article. Aye! but I *love its being long*. The things are usually so tantalizingly short.

always yrs
J C Powys

32

Saturday Oct 12th 1957.

My dear Friend and Best of all possible Professors

It would take a third story of Up & Out to do justice to the penetrating insight of those searching eyes of yours into my inmost soul. Aye! but and I'm *proud*—I can only pray not Vain & conceited too!—to be the subject of this amazing essay!

I am puzzled why I deliberately inserted that 'and' after 'but' following aye! It must have been a reversion to some *very* local dialectical habit in Derbyshire: Thats the only way I can explain it! but I know I wanted to support, prop up, strengthen, build in, the *'I'm proud'*!

O but I am so delighted with this discourse of yours on me. It couldnt be better. You sure have 'got my number'—you make me think *of one* of the divine songs of Paul Robeson the Negro whom the American Authorities for reasons that Id give a lot to know won't allow out of America. Its the song called *'There's a man going round taking names'* Well you, old friend, are 'a man *going round taking souls.'*

Nobody but you has brought into an analysis of me as a writer the one essential thing—namely that I was born a sadist! Not until *all sex-urge ended for good* on my 80th birthday or round about then, did sadism give place to the happiest of all the epochs of my life, the one I am enjoying now—which I know I am being absolutely correct in calling *Second-Childhood*. Here at this window on this couch with the broad window-sill as my desk on which are a picture of my mother two pictures of my old brother Littleton, a picture of my mother's mother *as a girl* and a picture of Princess Marie Louise saluting the audience at Foyle's Lunch about a week before she died, I *am daily being* waved to—forgive me for not getting down the Dictionary to see if it is *spelt waived* to?—by tiny toddlers between *1 and a half* and *3 and a half* And it interests me to note that boy toddlers waggle their hands as I do but girl-toddlers hold up their hands exactly as the Princess does in this picture *with the palm* towards the person to whom they are waving or acknowledging a wave!

Yes Sadism has always been my supreme temptation— The wickedest thing I ever did was in an Arbour in Norfolk when everybody was in Church and I chopped up with my pen-knife about 20 earth worms— And I well remember how at Lulworth (to which bay my father had once rowed me from Weymouth when so far old Littleton was unborn) when I was at the Prep at Sherborne where Powys Minor was always saving Powys

1 John Cowper Powys in the late 1950s at 1 Waterloo, Blaenau Ffestiniog

2 John Cowper Powys in the 1960s
at 1 Waterloo, Blaenau Ffestiniog

3 John Cowper Powys in the 1930s
at Rats Barn, E. Chaldon, Dorset

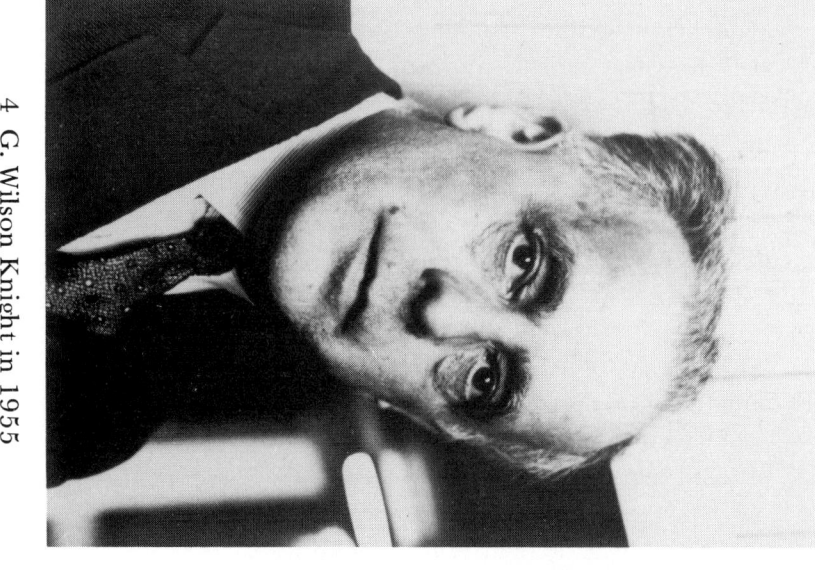

4 G. Wilson Knight in 1955

5 G. Wilson Knight in the role of Timon of Athens, 1940

Major from bullies thinking to myself that to avoid Hell for my sadistic thoughts it was worth-while to make a *faint struggle against them*! **Now** *I know* that the God of Christians is the most Sadistic God that has ever been worshipped! Recently entertaining a great friend and a deeply religious man I actually spat into the air 3 times & told him that I spat in the face of God!

Yes I read, and always liked, Davidson—just as I liked the Catholic Francis Thompson or is it Thomson and that *other one* (was he a Thomson or Thompson too?) who wrote the *City of Dreadful Night*—'There is no God. No Fiend with names divine made us to torture us. If we *must* pine, it is to satiate no Being's gall!' There's no 'p' is there in *"Thomson's Seasons"* which was my favourite poem when I was young.

O my dear Professor there will never be another plunge into the depths of my soul like this of your super or subter or inter penetrating eyes! Aye! you *are* a one! Lucky are all your pupils! As a Prof who is also a psychiatrist and who is also a prophet and one who can put religion Theology as well as Science, *where they Belong* there's none like you!

I wish the spirit of my old Nurse when I was young could visit me so that I could ask her about you! She used to teach me all about those 'bumps' that so tickled the fancy of Elia. I would ask *what it means* in your handwriting that every line from *John* to North Wales of an *address* as the one on this card *leaps up* more highly, more highly *towards the sky or the top on the right*, as I read the address? up! up! *North Wales*. [arrows

F

pointing to the top right surround *North Wales*]

 Your devoted old Boswell & P.P. joins in respectful love

J. C. P.

33

Tuesday Oct 15 1957.

My dear Professor

 I don't want to weary you with too often repeated praise & gratitude but I must tell you how deeply my Phyllis is delighted with this perfect analysis of her old John's nature and work and life.

 I warrant you are, just as I am, well! I *know* it from your writings, especially impressed by the *insight* that women are *sometimes* by no means always! able to express—But my Phyllis *was* able to express what she felt about this *Times Lit Sup* Essay on me! And a man's best girl for 33 years can come to know something about her companion's weaknesses and inspirations, his faults & virtues. She is going to try & get from Smith's Book-Shop here three or four more copies. I long to hear from our wonderful Boss of Macdonalds our Mr Eric Harvey who has been so ill with my old trouble of Deuodenal ulces but we heard from his wife that he is better and out again but whether back at the office yet I don't know. I can't help rather hoping *not* till he is quite strong & fit again but aye! I do so long for him to read this *Times Lit Sup*; but perhaps he *has* already. O

I am so proud of it!

Always your grateful
old John

34

Tuesday Oct 22nd 1957.

My dear Friend

For a Friend *indeed* art thou my dear Professor. Yes it would be just simply to omit one of the dominant personal urges in my whole life to omit or as you so Truly say to slur over *Sadism*. And I have found that our old family friend Louis Umfraville Wilkinson who had a devoted friendship for Llewelyn exactly like that of Achilles and Patroklus for Louis is so absolutely normal that his knowledge of the abnormalities of each member of our family is flawless. He could see, for instance, what nobody but you could see, what an interesting element of masochism exists in every real Sadist.

O you are so right my friend when you say that we shall never get these things straight if we don't talk freely and openly about them.

Far the saddest thing that has happened in our little circle of friends is the recent death of Louis' wife (his 4th wife) Joan. Everyone who met her or got to know her at all felt they'd found a girl who understood them and tenderly and exquisitely considered them through and through.

O yes my dear friend I've often wondered why I

care so little for any modern poetry since the days of Francis Thompson and John Davidson and W.B. Yeats. In those days an absolute and terrifying Simplicity was the note. 'As I came thro' the Desert, thus it was, as I came thro' the Desert'—'There is no God; no fiend with names divine made us to torture us—If we *must* pine, it is to satiate no Being's gall!'

And those lines of Yeats; just think how impossible it w^d be for a modern poet to write them . . .

> 'And in a far-off gentle valley stopping
> cried all my story to the dewdrops glistening
> but naught they heard for they are always listening,
> the dewdrops, to the sound of their own dropping.'[5]

The two Books I used to carry in my pocket—*each of them* for about two years—were Routledge's little small edition of *Whitman* and a small volume—I've forgotten the publisher—of Hazlitt's Essays . . . the former when I was still at College and the latter when I had begun earning my living as a lecturer at girl's schools in Hove in Brighton and in Eastbourne.

The Elderly Spinster Mistresses of Girl's Schools together with my own *Aunts* and *Great-Aunts* have been all my life second to my parents the greatest teachers I have ever had since Mr W.B. Wildman our House Master and 5th Form Master at Sherborne. That is why I have always had a mania for King Numa's *Egeria* or *Nymph in Antro* at Rome. I think Aspasia played that role at Athens too. That's why, I am sure, the Catholics have beaten the Puritans and Evangelicals. They saw the necessity of adding to Paul's Invention of Xtianity with its *Three Persons* a 4th *Person* namely 'Our Lady' who for all her fondness for the 'Holy Babe' grows more and more and more *like an Aunt* a wise Aunt to this mad cruel world! When the Babe became a bit too prominent our natural human craving for a *spinster auntie* appears in St Anne the Virgin's *Mummy*!

Aye! my dear Master, but what a task you have set for yourself in *British Drama* commissioned by *Phoenix House*. Ive just got to that touching figure in the Iliad *old man Phoenix* who from Achilles' childhood has been his teacher & tutor. This old gent is much more like one of my *Spinster Aunties* than any conceivable uncle!

Yes *Mr Foster White* of Macdonald's has from the start been a friend of mine. I hope one day he may take it into his head to visit North Wales. His favourite holiday place like that of all our family is Weymouth & Portland & Chesil Beach.

No dont 'ee bother to send us any of your copies of that precious unequalled *Times Lit Sup* because Phyllis *has ordered* 4 *more* of them at *Smith's* in this little town.

Yes I am like you rather partial to the Archbishop of York just as I am to Matthews, is he Dean of Westminster, whose sermons I read.

Yrs always always—& my Phyllis says the same—
old John

35

Tuesday Oct 29th 1957.
No! my dear friend I certainly do fully understand

your not wanting to extend your Professorship into the realms of *Administration*. I suppose among the great Poets very few have handled this practical side of ruling. I suppose Milton did under Cromwell and I suppose Goethe did under Karl August at Weimar—Dante certainly didnt or they wouldnt have pointed at him in the streets as the man who had been down to Hell and Horace refused point-blank & hurried away to his farm and his girls when Augustus asked him to be his Secretary!

 I am constantly being uplifted with inspired encouragement whenever the thought of your Article or Lecture for its much more exciting than any ordinary essay comes into my mind. And that happens often for all my best friends are discovering it and Phyllis *has ordered* & I hope we shall get three or four or five more copies.

 It is wonderfully exciting to me to think of your dealing with that epoch of Drama. Phyllis & I quarrel very much with *Marlowe* for making *his* Faust cringe & bow & scrape and howl & wriggle with humiliation at the end! How much better is Goethe's end—*Everything* is a **Symbol**—you feel that Goethe had known how to keep God & the Devil in their place ever since at six years old he listened to the news of the earthquake at *Lisbon*.

 O I am so glad you saw the Berry couple. I wonder how he'll work out that game of Chess of poetry with its grammatical pawns & knights & castles!

 What goes on striking me most constantly & most deeply as I struggle with the Iliad is its absolutely astonishing *domestic* and *family reproductions* again and again and again of *the home life we all know still changed hardly at all in three thousand years*! These Greeks & Trojans and their Olympian friends on both sides— though they are always piercing each other with spears and cutting off each others' arms & legs—reproduced with complete and deep deep deep understanding the ways of men and women and of their servants and of their lads and maidens and their lords and kings and governments and wise prophets and priests in a way that is O *so like what happens today*!! Shakespeare is always a Prospero who sees that we are the stuff *that dreams are made on* and our little life is rounded with a sleep. But that is the view of a Sage, a Seer, a psychic Visionary. But the realism of Homer has something in *its eternal ordinariness* different from that. But Shakespeare and Homer are alike in the strange way in which both their private personal identities *cease to exist*. We dont know who they are! The stream of tendency that makes for righteousness has now hundreds of boats on its waters and divers below its water it is as if the human race itself said 'come now—to *hell with 'Great Men'*—let us see what happens when we all autobiographize together for once not excluding our cooks and black smiths and kitchen-maids and *great-aunts*!

Well my dear friend I bet your Drama Book will fill that gap in space that all of us are always struggling to fill! *So long*! and all our Best *from both*

always your old
J C P.

JOHN COWPER POWYS TO WILSON KNIGHT

36

Nov 6th 1957.

I am so interested in all you say my dear friend about your Drama Book. I know so little about Ben Jonson that I cannot debate or even dispute with you about his merits. It keeps coming into my head that he 'Trailed' or *'carried a Pike'* in the war against the Spaniards in the Netherlands and the *tune*—I dont know *how old that tune* is!—of *'Drink to me only with thine eyes'* is one of 'those things' that I say to myself when I *am going* to *sleep*! Not to *make* myself go to sleep for *that* is never necessary! but to make myself *enjoy going to sleep* more still for it is always my greatest enjoyment of every day, yes! even *a little more still*! I wrote to a friend the other day and told him how intensely I longed for *Annihilation* and I was amazed how *shocked* he was! It isn't that I dont enjoy my life—Indeed I sincerely hope I'll live to be 90 if not 95 like this poor Marquis of Winchester—but I dont see that you cant enjoy this life very much indeed while at the same time you enjoy extremely the thought of annihilation. I prefer *'annihilation'* even to the *'sleep of death'*; for how do we know that, as Science can take dogs into space and catapult them out of space it cant play all sorts of *resurrection tricks* on a *dead body* as that youth did in Mrs Shelley's Frankenstein?

No this old age is *far the happiest part of my life*—Well! if that's so isn't it natural that I don't want to go

thro' all the labour and effort of *another life*?
    Aye! but I cant wait to enjoy your *Drama Book*.
                            Yrs always
                            J C Powys

37

Friday November 15th 1957.
My dear Friend—O what an interesting & provocative letter this is from you! What I have now come to feel, but I know very well it *may* be simply the result of what I love to call my present second-childhood, is simply a longing for absolute annihilation; not at all because I am not enjoying my life *as it is*. In fact if I could go on *as I am* with Miss Phyllis Playter to take care of me I would be perfectly happy to look forward to living *ten more years*—that is till I were 95 like old Eden Phillpotts and my old Cousin Catharine in Norwich who tho' totally deaf and totally blind dictates to one or other of her 'baby-sitters' or 'old-lady sitters' *such* witty & lively letters to me. I've got pictures of both these Ninety-Fivers and while poor old Phillpotts' face is is criss-crossed with lines in a way that is saddening to see my old Catharine's face is gay & lively and without a line and yet her photo has only just been taken by her son as she reads a volume of *BRAIL* if I spell that correctly! I must have often boasted to you about her for on her father's side she is descended directly from Donne and on her mother's from the brother of *Anne Bullen* or *Bolleyne* is it?—O No I would love *under present con-*

ditions to live ten more years for I am greatly enjoying my old age which is *far* the happiest portion of my life, O yes! *far,* far, *far*!

But I am, as this *funny modern phrase* has it, *panicked* by the idea of any after-life *of any kind at all*. What I feel in my inmost self which depends entirely on my outmost sensations is that though I love my present life so well that I'd willingly live to be **100 as I am** I *dont want* the very nicest life I can imagine once this is over! But I love to think of all of us *'Buana-Powysies'* as the Blacks of Kenya call my only surviving brother William who alone of the ranch-men has never been attacked by the Mau-Mau because like *all* the *six sons* of our parents he has got in him something of the *simple cunning* of oxen and asses and rhinoceruses and hippopotamusies which *must mark* the true *Iberians* from North Africa. Wales is full of lots of other Celtic tribes but I tend to think that we've got something of that son of Noah, called 'Ham' in *our* deepest veins!

My dreams are always of the same kind *an exciting story*. Last night I dreamed that my son's uncle *Harry Lyon* had a son which he never had & Phyllis & I kept him hidden in a tiny turret next the room in which we slept!

O I shall love seeing your Review of Llewelyn's book. As a reader I greatly prefer him to myself because of his complete absorbtion in his subject—I forget whether absorbtion has any ps in it! whereas I've got a vein of quick-moving *cleverness* in me which none of my brothers have and which is a very very very Un-Powysian characteristic.

I love to think of your talking of my books at the University of Hull— My old friend Redwood-Anderson taught in some School there for a long time before he & his wife separated & he came to Corwen. He has now married a beautiful young wife who has given him back five years at least of his life! And they live in the Summer for a few months near here but most of the year at Sible Hedingham Essex in a house belonging to his beautiful new wife. He has been for years and years at work on an exhaustive history of *English Metre* in poetry. He has published, by my publisher Macdonald, a volume of poems called *'Almanac'* about the Seasons of our year, and he is still working on his Metre book and also on a book of his own Philosophy. I think he's about 77.

Always your old
J. C. Powys

38

[*No date: postmarked* 3 Dec 57]

My dear Friend

both Phyllis & I are thrilled by your words about Llewelyn and I think you brought me in most happily and Truly & to the point. You sure *are* one for hitting the mark in these Critical Contests. There's nobody like you 'at thik little job'

I am delighted by this word of fine praise for The Brazen Head from your poet-friend *Tom Blackburn* & I thank you my dear old friend for letting [me?] keep his letter.

This is by my soul a wonderful little description of Ll's way of writing. It couldn't have been put better— Phyllis has cut it out to send to Alyse Gregory his widow, who oddly enough has been staying with a friend in Exeter! whence you have just come back to work!

We are now sending to you as a Xmas offering that translation of the *Mabinogion* which Lady Charlotte *once did* so well as our two Professors fully admit here in *this new* translation of theirs— You'll see how I beg them by the Styx to swear to keep their word with Everyman, as Sleep begs Hera to keep *her word* about giving him as his wife Pasithea, the youngest of the Graces, whom he has longed for, *all his days*! Iliad XIV line 271. Think of a girl having Sleep as her bridegroom!

What you say about annihilation only affecting the person himself but *not* something else of which he is the temporary embodiment is a striking idea but I don't want to be as someone said, 'surrounded by spirit.'

Always your old
J.C.P.

39

Thursday Dec 12th 1957.

My dear Friend

O how absolutely right you are about sex being a hidden secret power running like the sap of a tree thro' all the branches of our Tree of Life! I love your invented word *aurafied.* I wonder how it came about that *air* and *gold* to the Romans were so closely allied? Here's what my little Follett's (Chicago) Latin Dictionary says—

aura   air, gentle breeze, breath, wind, odour, exhalation
aurarius   golden
auratus   gilt
auriolus   golden

and then comes the word for **ear**

auricula   ear-lap (does that mean the part ladies have pierced?)
and *auris* ear

and then *aurigo* chariotier or **helmsman**!
and finally *aurora* dawn
and *aurum* gold.

Isn't that a significant alliance, this nearness of *air, ear,* and *gold*? I bet it filled the enemies of the Roman Legions with **awe**!

    I love to think of your meeting your pupils entering Oxford & Cambridge and I am mighty proud, old friend, that you've put my works into their hands & heads as Zeus was always sending his son Hermes-Argieiphontes with his golden sandals and his Magic Wand to help the young men . . . *and the very old men too* . . . as when in the shape of a handsome young Myrmydon Myrmidon he helped old Priam and the old Herald to get . . . to get safe unseen in the darkness through the Greek huts till they reached the hut of Achilles *near which* kept *unspoilt* in spite of the vindictiveness of Achilles by the carefulness of Apollo who was one of the Gods most strongly on the side of the Trojans lay the corpse of Hector.

JOHN COWPER POWYS TO WILSON KNIGHT

What a comfort for your Christmas will be with your own people in your own home in Exeter! Whereas for my poor Phyllis, having to consider her relatives in America as well my friends & relations over here, it will be as if it were the Birthday not of Jesus but of Judas if not of the *devil*! I'll address this scrawl to *Caroline House* to await *arrival*.

Yrs with great gratitude for your encouragement carries me along

John C. Powys

V
The Last Letters
1958-1962

The pace slows, inevitably—eleven letters in the final five years as against eighteen in 1957—and the handwriting shows a new shakiness. But the final three letters to Knight, written during Powys's ninetieth year, are fully as legible as the first, a quarter of a century earlier. There is some repeating; and yet grouping letters in a book magnifies the kind of repetitions present in the letters of everyone who does not keep carbon copies of all he has said before.

Powys continued to write fiction—to tell tales— until the time this correspondence stops, some thirteen months before his death on June 17, 1963. Two of these late stories, Real Wraiths *and* Two & Two, *were published in 1974 by Jeffrey Kwintner of the Village Press, London. And there were tributes: the award, in 1958, from the Hamburg Free Academy of Arts described by Knight in Appendix 2, and special 'Powys Issues' of three journals:* Dock Leaves *(later* The Anglo-Welsh Review), *Vol. 7, No. 19, Spring 1956;* New Chapter, *Vol. 1, No. 3, in September 1958; and* A Review of English Literature, *Vol. 4, No. 1, in January 1963.*

But Powys never read the ultimate tribute from G. Wilson Knight, written in January 1959, and reproduced here as Appendix 2: Knight's nomination of John Cowper Powys for the Nobel Prize in Literature.

40

May 20, 1958.

My dear Professor and best of friends

I heard the *Cuckoo* today—I have only heard it *once before* this year and that was on Friday the Second of May.

I sent your grand long article on me in the *Times Lit Sup* to a Hindoo called Kewal Motwani of Ceylon who is writing a treatise on my work but I told him that the articles in the Times Lit Sup were anonymous. O I am so proud, my dear friend that you gave a talk on my books to some Exeter University students and that it went so well. Yes our old family friend Louis Wilkinson took such a lot of trouble over those Letters especially over the *Index*! Think of having an *Index* to one man's letters to another man! Louis's Mother was a great friend of my Mother and Theodore went to Louis's Father's School in Aldeburgh Suffolk.

I am proud, my dear Professor, of the fact that you wrote something, never mind how short, on me for this new Magazine called New Chapter.

No I never read Browning on *Lazarus resurrected*—and how for him big things were levelled with little things.

Aye! my dear friend, but Phyllis & I cant control our delight in thinking of your bringing your unique insight to bear on the Mabinogion.

'The Meaning of Culture' has just been brought out by some Japanese Publishers with wonderful notes in English and Japanese by an old correspondent of mine

Professor Ichiro Hara of Tokyo.[1] So what with Kewal Motwani in Ceylon and Ichiro Hara in Tokyo I'm advancing like the old Prince Madoc from Port-Madoc into the Orient! You know they say—for Prince Madoc never came home—that some tribe of Red Indians still talk a sort of Welsh!

You really *are* a one, Professor, reading for your *drama book*, dramas *you've never* so much as heard of! Heavens! but this *will* be a book to fill a gap in our literary Horizon!

All the best from us both old friend—
Your J. C. P.

41

Monday, July 14, 1958.

My dear Friend and most powerful of all my literary supports here's the address of the writer and lecturer in Ceylon with whom I have corresponded for many a year

Kewal Motwani
6 Claessnen Place
Colombo 4
Ceylon

Another oriental correspondent of mine for an even longer time is

Ichiro Hara
59 Miyamae-cho
Meguro-Ku
Tokyo
Japan

The former has written a good long article or little paper booklet on my work but the latter has got a Japanese Publisher to publish in two excellently printed little paper volumes my 'Meaning of Culture' with elaborate notes in Japanese.

I am delighted my dear friend with this wonderful review of yours of my Letters to Louis Wilkinson. Whatever success this book may have (and it really does seem to have made a hit with all my friends) is due to *Louis*. Think of making such a careful *Index* and such excellent notes and all for the letters of one old friend to another!

I've got a wonderful photo of my brother Theodore, copied or photographed from Augustus John's portrait of him. So two of the Brothers Powys will be seen by the next and the next generation as this great artist saw them!

O he is such a large-hearted and generous man—I do admire him so, not only as a genius and painter but as a person. Phyllis and I were simply thrilled by his visit. In appearance he is exactly like Zeus.

I am delighted to hear what you say about my being allowed to tell my Ceylon friend and Japanese friend that you were the author of these anonymous pages in the *Times. Lit. Sup.*

O yes my niece the daughter of A.R. Powys has just visited Phyllis and me here and she told us she had met your young disciple *Campion* whom you brought here.

Yes Phyllis Playter and your old J C Powys were as you can imagine both honored & scared by that Presentation of the Bronze Plaque from Hamburg. I lectured in

Hamburg (I don't know a word of German) when I was 22 & had just got my degree. The President of the Academy was not allowed to travel *by his doctor* so the Secretary of the Academy *Rolf Italiaander* brought it. He was a very nice man and a very easy man to get on with, and we both liked him very much.

 I dont know when my Iliad book called Homer and the AEther will come out but its in Macdonald's hands and Ive got the advance Royalty. I am now *half way through* a story about natives in the remotest star in the Milky Way a story I have named *All or Nothing.*

 All the best from us both old friend your ever grateful

J. C. Powys

42

Tuesday, Sept. 9th 1958.

My dear Professor

 Yes I've kept your 3^d stamp for use when I've got your Book which I am greatly looking forward to receive. Its a funny thing but I've never read *nor did I know it existed* till everybody nowadays is writing about it—this Henry VIII by Shakespeare!

 Aye! but I am longing to read your Book and you can bet I shan't miss those notes where there's a reference to 'little me'!

 But I already have a strong telepathic or psychic intimation that I shall recognize and give myself up to & agree wholeheartedly with what you say about the

Crown & christianity!

 I *know* I'll want to keep the Book when it comes. Aye! but I'm so looking forward to it.

 I am glad you have quoted Gordon Craig for I have a queer regard for him owing to my devotion to Irving & Ellen Terry when I was young. Its queer what a prejudice I have against G.B. Shaw! But all of us devoted readers of poetry have funny prejudices! My mother brought me up on Tennyson and still the poets I love quoting best after Shaspeare & Milton are Horace and Tennyson!

 No more till it comes! always your your old
John C. Powys.

43

[Postcard]   [Postmarked: 19 Sep 58]
The Sovereign Flower has come—I'll write when I have studied it a bit.
Yrs
J C Powys

44

Wednesday, September 24th 1958.

My dear Professor

 I have been absolutely absorbed in this Book of yours—reading it *very slowly* & trying to absorb all its profound and subtle suggestions.

THE LAST LETTERS

Here are a few of the sentences upon which I have meditated the most.

Page 57 [53] Timon's Swift-like loathing of humanity's sillinesses and excesses.

Page 65 The overthrowing of a male-value by a Female Force which condemns from a deeper wisdom man's dramatic ambition . . . Antony *versus* Cleopatra. *He* is masculinity personified—whereas *she* is expressly and universally feminine.

Page 66 Royalty draws near to erotic potency.

Page 68 Coriolanus brought to heel by his Mother.

Page 71 Prospero controls Ariel and Caliban as man's judgement must control both ethereal fancy and physical instinct.

Page 72 Prospero lives half in eternity and from that eminence sees beyond all temporal glories; and presses on yet further, beyond the different nihilisms of Macbeth and Timon into the Transience of the created universe itself.

True Royalty is precisely and only *poetry incarnate.*

Page 85 For a child eternity and time necessarily embrace and futurity lies curled.

Page 160 Out of the new Aquarian Age concerning which our esoteric thought today is never tired of prophesying and to which the feminine insistence of Shaw and O'Neill and O'Casey is always pointing, a new form of Society predicted and not only so but actually coming into being and in this new Society, thus created, Feminine Values will be in the ascendant.

Page 160 sequitur. The whole tendency of Shakespeare's Humanism counters the doctrine of Hell as a state of lasting torment after death.

In Nietzsche's *Birth of Tragedy* his Dionysian element may be equated *with* **our Spatial** element. They are both dynamic with a **thrust** to be regarded as *Vertical* rather than *Horizontal*. [254]

Nietzsche's system by bringing in the vertical or spiritual Dimension resolves our paradox. [255]

What we call Literature is a *Living Record* more vital than History and from certain writers who speak *for Britain* we may explore the Soul-Force from which her Power and Influence have grown. 'If poetry,' says Keats, 'doesn't come as naturally as leaves from a Tree it had better not come at all.' [266, 268]

We must think of Shakespeare in association with Queen Elizabeth—of Pope in association with Queen Anne—of Tennyson in association with Queen Victoria. [270]

The Crown is the personification of the Impersonal. It is the supreme paradox—the final source of power being lodged in the hands of one who has no power. [277]

Each play of Shakespeare's meaning for us must stand for the *creative impulse* behind the text which is responsible for the experience which each play gives us *as a whole*. We should give more detached attention to the individual peculiarities of style in each play. Each of the greater plays has its own unique atmosphere. Finally [in this list of suggestions from Knight] the Plays of Shakespeare demand

and provide the now so necessary synthesis of religious and aesthetic experience. [291, 293]

The 'streams of tendency' in *'The Sovereign Flower'* from which I myself draw most help for my private life are your magical and mystical ideas as to the Symbol of Royalty, borne out by Goethe's last words (aren't they) in *Faust*?—about everything we we see and feel being a *Symbol* of Something beyond life and death and everything else?— These in the first place and again to bring Goethe into it Damn! I can't spell the words! 'das ewig veibliche' the **Eternal Feminine**: O I do *so* agree with this! Yes! women *are* mysteriously wiser than men— Every girl is a Queen or a Princess Royal! But every man isn't a King or a Hero! The church—especially the Catholic church—has tried to steal this Mystery of Royalty and apply it to the *Priesthood*! But they can't do it! What Image remains before the eyes of all of us ordinary heathen when a Priest has been lecturing us? The Holy Father Pius the Twelfth? *No*! Though I think myself that he's our greatest man alive on earth at this moment. What then? *The Image of 'Our Lady'*! Yes! *any* little wretched Icon or picture with that Mother of us all upon it! I am anything but a Christian—a polytheist perhaps? I dont know what I am—But when I see *Our Lady*—

Well I *must* stop! Good luck to you in all your work, my respected friend, We've been having torrents of rain!

Yrs always
J C Powys

45

Tuesday, May 5th 1959.

My dear Professor

How very good of you to send me these copies of your wonderful Review of my *Homer & the AEther* in *T.L.S.* And also the *Twentieth Century* one. I like to think of there being one too in the Yorkshire Post, similar to these.

Just think my dear Friend of your undertaking such a terrific task as the History of of Drama in this Country. What you say is certainly most interesting, that certain dramatists who have been allowed to fall into oblivion possess many of the qualities that are most admired in this present day.

O my dear Professor and wonderful friend it is of great interest to me to learn that Bernard Jones was a pupil of yours. I have had quite a correspondence with him of late for his association with old Barnes whom I remember so well when my Father was a Curate at St Peters in Dorchester.[2] We used to go to tea with him and I can see him now in my memory walking up and down the chestnut walks in those knee-breeches and silver-buckled shoes that he refused to relinquish for modern attire. Hardy was so good to me in those days. He used to take me up to his study and I can well recall seeing the original MSS of Tess. He taught me to admire Edgar Poe of whom I was quite ignorant before then. O yes I well remember Oliver Campion bring[ing] you to see us. But for heaven's sake Professor you must make him paint you again for your whole searching and penetrating genius is in your eyes. That look in them which both my Miss Playter and I have come to know so well and nobody else,—certainly no professor—possesses it or anything like it, has got all the psychic power which will make you known to posterity. We both like to think of your having this term's length as a time for writing your great book.

Well my dear Sir may all the gods bless you and keep you till we meet again and so says my Phyllis

Your forever grateful
J C Powys

46

Tuesday, July 5th 1960.

My dear Friend

It is indeed an exciting event to hear from you again. I wish the latest news that we—Miss Phyllis Playter still an American Citizen and your old John Cowper Powys can give you about ourselves were a bit more cheerful; but we have both been smitten by this mysterious thing they call *Asian Flue* though where the devil in Asia it comes from nobody seems able to say! My Miss Phyllis was hit first by it but she is better thank heaven now but I have been made so weak by it that I cant go out of this tiny house for the smallest little stroll as yet; though I *do* manage to climb up the eleven steps of of the little staircase from Phyllis's Parlor to my little reading and writing room—too small to be called a 'Study.' This I do every day about 5 in the afternoon & I stay up there till about ten in the evening when I come down & go to bed in the Parlor.

We had a very nice visit from my Publisher the Boss of Macdonalds & Co, where there are no Macdonalds left, a day or two ago. He has just brought out a new book of mine called *'All or Nothing.'*

Well, my dear Professor, I do hope you yourself, 'your wone self' as we say in Dorset are O.K. as we say in America.

[no signature]

47

[Postmarked: 1 Aug 1961]

My dear Friend

We are both, Miss Phyllis Playter and I, very pleased you lent Margaret Turner my 'Wood and Stone.' We are fond of her and have great confidence in her. We were indeed so glad to get this letter from you. We were amused by those small misprints you found such as *peotic* instead of *poetic*! And your Review in the Times Lit Sup which has been sent to us by lots of people has pleased us very much.

I have noted from your letter today that you have an article coming out in which you develop some of the ideas that particularly interested you in re-reading *'Wolf Solent'* & I look forward to reading it. I am fascinated by your idea of these *two Selves* within all of us, *one* for whom Death is the end; and the *other* for whom Death is the beginning.

THE LAST LETTERS

It is wonderful to me your having the Six Clerk [Clark] Lectures at Cambridge next year— And it was wise & good indeed of you to tell that lady who was asking for our address that she must get to know us first. I am sorry your great Book on Drama has been so long delayed. But I shall be interested in those two books you speak of—one on Christianity, and one on Ibsen. And now I see you have daringly connected yourself with these recent Byronic controversies, for I am now reading 'New Light on Byron' Thursday July 13th[3] —

     yrs ever & always
     John Cowper Powys

48

Nov. 23th 1961.

My dear Friend

I was very pleased to hear from you and very proud of what you said in your critical Essay about myself and Joyce and Lawrence.[4] Your letter in the Times Literary Supplement evidently delighted all my adherents and today someone has sent me this week's T.L.S. with two letters responding very much to what you said. You have certainly played your part in backing me up and I thank you from the bottom of my heart. You can imagine very well I am sure how my mind keeps reverting to my dead brothers and sisters and also to my brother William still safe in Kenya and my sisters Katie & Lucy still near each other in Dorset.

I hope Alan Sommers is getting on well. He impres-

sed us as being an especially sensitive and unusual young man. Remember us to him when you write to him.
Yours sincerely & affectionately
John Cowper Powys

49

December 1st 1961.
I have just received your cheque for Three Pounds from Macdonalds today [for permission to quote]. And it was very thoughtful of you to send it.
Phyllis has just got for me a fine warm sweater which I am wearing tonight for the first time and it is a great comfort so I will regard your cheque as making it a part-present from you. I expect this is a very busy time for you nearing the end of the term; so don't feel you must answer this or my other letter.
Yours affectionately & gratefully
John Cowper Powys

50

[Postmarked: 3 May 1962]
My dear Wilson Knight
I do indeed thank you very much for having your Book on English Drama sent to me. I do greatly appreciate it. I think at this time it is especially important to call to mind what we owe to the genius of the Past.
Every afternoon now I have got accustomed to walk-

ing up the hill behind my house to the Five Steps at the foot of our waterfall and then sitting down for a while on the northern side of the road to my left, where emerges against the sky and mountains the fore-front of our Welsh Woollen Mill.

I think it is wonderful how you get all these Books written, along with your work in the University.

Yrs always sincerely and faithfully
John Cowper Powys

[*Four months before his ninety-first birthday, John Cowper Powys died on June 17, 1963.*]

Notes

NOTES TO THE INTRODUCTION

1 For a typical sermon by his father, the Rev. Charles Francis Powys, Vicar of Montacute, see *Powys Newsletter—Three* (Hamilton, N.Y., 1973).
2 My transcription of the original letter differs from Malcolm Elwin's in *Letters to His Brother Llewelyn*, volume 1, London, 1975, primarily in punctuation and the recording of italics.
3 A name used by the childhood triumvirate, his sister Marian and his brothers Bertie (Albert Reginald) and Lulu (Llewelyn). The series of dots are Powys's punctuation; elipses within square brackets indicate my omissions from these long paragraphs.
4 For press reactions, see *Shakespearian Production*, pp. 313-16.

NOTES TO CHAPTER ONE

1 The concern was justified; several years later Powys lost the use of one eye.
2 Knight's essay on Francis Berry is reprinted in *Neglected Powers*. Berry's 'Fall of a Tower' is published in *The Galloping Centaur* (Methuen & Co., London, 1952; reissued 1970). Other poetic volumes by Berry are *Morant Bay* and *Ghosts of Greenland* (Routledge & Kegan Paul, London, 1961 and 1966). His sonnet 'For John Cowper Powys on his Ninetieth Birthday' was printed in

Notes to Chapters One and Two

Derek Langridge's *John Cowper Powys: A Record of Achievement* (The Library Association, London, 1966); and his essay 'J.C. Powys and Romance' in *Essays on John Cowper Powys*, edited by Belinda Humfrey (University of Wales Press, Cardiff, 1972). He has recently published an historical novel, *I Tell of Greenland* (Routledge & Kegan Paul, 1977).
3 Knight's brother. W.F. Jackson Knight, published *Roman Vergil* in 1944. The generous payment was for permission to quote from Powys's *Rabelais* in G. Wilson Knight's book on Pope, *Laureate of Peace*.
4 Forty years earlier Powys lectured on *Timon of Athens* while he was a Cambridge University Extension Lecturer. Knight comments on this forgetfulness in *Neglected Powers*, p. 166.

NOTES TO CHAPTER TWO

1 John Cowper Powys's ashes were scattered at Chesil Beach. The misspellings—Beach Tree and numerolgical—are Powys's.
2 On leaving Cambridge, Powys's grandfather became Rector of Stalbridge in Dorset. The 'young widow,' Powys's grandmother, had a daughter from her first marriage, Philippa Knight, who was John Cowper Powys's god-mother. Philippa married Walter Waddington Shirley, D.D., Regius Professor of History at Oxford. Two of their five children, Alice and Ralph, figure later in this correspondence.
3 In 1964, on a copy of this letter, Knight wrote: 'I was intending to use the name, which had been planned

for me before baptism but was rejected to avoid the sequence "G.W.R." [commonly used for Great Western Railway]. There was nothing very new in this intention, since my first letter in *The Times Literary Supplement* on 23 December 1926 was signed "G.W.R. Knight." Neither then nor later did the intention mature, because of the attendant complications.' But in the nineteen-seventies, on officially taking the name *Richard*, he placed it between George and Wilson—G.R.W. Knight.

4 Littleton Alfred Powys, born 31 August 1902. He converted to Roman Catholicism after World War Two, in which he had served as an Anglican Chaplain with the rank of Captain. John Cowper Powys and Margaret Lyon, the sister of Harry Lyon, Powys's close friend at Cambridge, were married on 9 April 1896, after a one-year engagement. They became estranged during his years of lecturing in America; he contributed to her support until her death in 1947. Powys's brother Theodore, author of *Mr Weston's Good Wine* and many other novels, died on 17 November 1953, at the age of seventy-seven.

5 Reviewed by Knight in *The Yorkshire Post*, 26 May 1954. See also *Neglected Powers*, pp. 365-7.

6 The three-act play was produced by Arnold Freeman at Sheffield, and published by the author at Leeds in October 1954. The most recent production was by the BBC in December 1974.

7 A misprint in Knight's *Laureate of Peace*.

8 His 81st. Littleton was born in 1874, eighteen months after John.

9 Knight's essay on Arnold's 'The Scholar Gipsy' is reprinted in *Neglected Powers*. It appeared originally in

Notes to Chapters Three and Four

The Review of English Studies, January 1955.

NOTES TO CHAPTER THREE

1 Many friends through the years tried to convince Powys to be less conscientious about answering every letter he received.
2 W.F. Jackson Knight's translation of *The Aeneid*.
3 *Lucifer*: page 36, line 15—*than*, not *that*; page 152, line 19—*be*, not *by*.
4 The key word, tantalizingly missing here, is given in capital letters at the very beginning of the next letter—before the date and salutation—in response to Knight's query. The noun *sadism* fits less well than *sadistic* or *auto-erotic*, but Powys, of course, did not have his own letter at hand.
5 Spelled *Dom* first, then *Don*.

NOTES TO CHAPTER FOUR

1 Robert V. Lancaster's unpublished edition of the later letters of Powys to Louis Wilkinson shows that he wrote forty-seven times to Wilkinson in 1957.
2 Raymond Garlick, who lived in Blaenau Ffestiniog, prepared a tribute to Powys for presentation on the BBC Welsh Home Service on 27 June 1957, using scripts from a number of friends. Powys himself turned down several invitations to speak on the radio. Related, perhaps, to his dislike for seeing himself in a mirror are his consistent refusals to be broadcast or recorded. Garlick edited a special Powys issue of *Dock Leaves* in 1956.

3 Alan Sommers, author of a provocative article on *Titus Andronicus*, 'Wilderness of Tigers', in *Essays in Criticism*, July 1960, X, 3.
4 *Jobber Skald*, the title of the first English edition (1935) of *Weymouth Sands* (New York, 1934), was translated into French by Marie Canavaggia.
5 Yeats wrote 'The Sad Shepherd' in the third person, for the most part; the shepherd 'cried all his story' to the dewdrops that are always listening 'for the sound of their own dropping'.

NOTES TO CHAPTER FIVE

1 Professor Hara continues his devoted scholarship; scheduled for Japanese publication in 1978 was a translation of *A Philosophy of Solitude* and his book about Powys. The winter 1978 issue of *The Powys Newsletter* (Hamilton, New York) reprints the introduction John Cowper Powys wrote in 1958 for the two volumes *Culture and Life* and *Culture and Nature* (drawn from *The Meaning of Culture*).
2 From 1879 to 1885, after leaving Shirley, Derbyshire, and before becoming Vicar of Montacute. 'Old Barnes' is William Barnes, 1801-1886, poet and Rector of Came, a hamlet near Thomas Hardy's Max Gate home on the south-east side of Dorchester. Bernard Jones edited *The Poems of William Barnes* (1962), *John Cowper Powys: Letters to Glyn Hughes* (1971), and *Romer Mowl and Other Stories* by John Cowper Powys (1974).
3 The date of Knight's review article in *The Yorkshire Post*.

Notes to Chapter Five

4   In *Essays in Criticism*, XI (October 1961). Knight's letter to *The Times Literary Supplement*, 17 November 1961, expressed the 'strongest possible agreement' with the statement in an earlier letter from 'an American correspondent' (George Steiner, then teaching in the United States): 'The failure of all but a handful of English readers and critics to perceive that John Cowper Powys stands beside Hardy and D.H. Lawrence among the masters is a scandal'. Subsequent issues of *The Times Literary Supplement* carried letters from others who agreed with Knight and Steiner.

Appendices

In *Neglected Powers*, speaking of the possible publication of his letters from John Cowper Powys, Wilson Knight said:

It is my wish that, if published, they should appear only as a complete and unexpurgated set (48 letters, 2 cards), together with the spirit-communication of 1963 and my letter on Powys to the Nobel Committee of 15 January 1959. (161)

It seems also important to reprint his essay-review of *Up and Out*, 'Cosmic Correspondences', of which Powys could say, after its appearance in *The Times Literary Supplement* of 11 October 1957, 'there will never be another plunge into the depths of my soul like this.' The essay, a prime example of Knight's ability to go to the 'imaginative core' of a man's life work, is printed with the permission of *The Times Literary Supplement* and Routledge & Kegan Paul, whose slightly revised version in *Neglected Powers* I follow. *Psychic News* permits the use of their story of the spirit-communication from their No. 1625, dated 27 July 1963.

Appendix 1

Cosmic Correspondences

Of his two new stories *Up and Out* and *The Mountains of the Moon* (published together in 1957 under the title of the first) John Cowper Powys writes:

> The feeling, for it is more than a doctrine or an idea, underlying both these stories, is that there is nothing in the universe devoid of some mysterious element of consciousness, however small, queer, ridiculous, or whether animal, vegetable or mineral, such a thing may be.*

This feeling pervades all Powys's writings, and it is perhaps this that has held up the understanding of them. He has been writing now for more than forty years and during the past twenty-five his output has been prodigious; and yet, though authentic voices have never been wanting to assert his genius, the prevailing critical mood of the past two generations has been strangely lethargic in response.

Many subsidiary reasons could be given. The difficulties of James Joyce, serious as they are, are just such as appeal to the twentieth-century literary mind, which loves nothing so much as a puzzle; and as for D.H. Lawrence, though his more esoteric intuitions are not always easy to assimilate, yet his approach, the kinetic descriptions, the nervous, fiery impressionism, the hammering repetitions, the speed, the social attack, all are on the wavelength of our 'age of anxiety'.

Powys is never obscure, and his large works, with their long and classically modulated periods, their wealth of vocabulary and allusion, their strange assurance and utter independence of what most of us would say that he ought to be writing, pursue us with the unhurrying and unperturbed pace of Francis Thompson's God in 'The

---

*This was, if I recall correctly, a note on the jacket. It is not in the book.

Cosmic Correspondences

Hound of Heaven'. Escape has proved impossible, and we are today watching the steady rise to full recognition of one of the outstanding writers of our century. But that recognition must in part depend, too, on an understanding of the more deeply seated reason for the reluctance which some readers have felt in face of even such obviously great novels as *A Glastonbury Romance* (1933) and *Jobber Skald* (1935; as *Weymouth Sands*, 1963). This deeper reason will hardly be elucidated by any study of the history of the novel; it is far closer to the histories of mythology and poetry. Little enough divides Powys's rich deployment of Biblical and Greek mythology in his recently published poetic narrative *Lucifer* (1956; composed 1906) from the prose descriptions of his novels.

The myths and legends of all races, with their fauns, dryads and nymphs, their trolls and fairies, have from earliest times asserted the spiritual properties of natural phenomena; and in our own literature we can watch a reliance on such 'personifications' gradually giving way to the more explicit doctrines of a Blake or a Wordsworth, and the deliberate dramatization of Earth's awakening in response to Man's liberation in Shelley's *Prometheus Unbound*. But, except for Carlyle's *Sartor Resartus* and John Davidson's prophetic asseverations in both prose and poetry in the early years of this century, there has been little more, in England, of power and authenticity until Lawrence and Powys; and of these two, whereas Lawrence's non-human vitalism concentrated mainly, and with a success matched in our literature by Byron alone, on the higher, dynamic animals, Powys's favourite concen-

Cosmic Correspondences

tration falls on the lower orders: on the reptilian kinds, and insects; on plant-life, trees and earth; and on minerals. To him the humblest variety of unnoticed vegetation is an actor in his drama, and from his first novel *Wood and Stone* (U.S.A., 1915) onwards stone is impregnated, continually, with a spiritual significance.

Such intuitions are not new. The total wisdom, the cosmic consciousness, expressed, in which you begin to feel that the vibrations of man's little story are responsive to, and may in turn affect, not only the earth itself but the farthest star, has been embedded in occult teaching for centuries; astrology is merely one symptom of it, just as mythology is another. Both Lawrence and Powys search back to the ancient world: Lawrence to the Etruscans and the mythological traditions of the Aztecs, Powys to the Greeks and the Celtic records of *The Mabinogion*. It is a wisdom often lost, and always hard to capture in direct consciousness. It is not necessarily un-Christian: it may be said to be implied by Hooker's doctrine of immanence in the *Ecclesiastical Polity*, and it is certainly true that nature is being regarded *sacramentally*. The magical, animistic understanding has been alive, beneath the academic surface, in many periods, and nearly always in poetry; as today in the work of Edith Sitwell. At present its main supporters, outside the various schools of admittedly occult tradition, are our imaginative writers, and whenever from time to time a work of more explicit and scientific formulation, such as Sir Francis Younghusband's *The Living Universe*, appears, it is quickly forgotten, there being no official guardianship for such studies.

Cosmic Correspondences

A considerable responsibility falls accordingly on our literary consciousness. The critical temper of our time has been countered by Middleton Murry's life-long, if indecisive, attempt, from his own mystical experience—as recounted in his book *God*—onwards, to relate the mystical fact to poetic truth; and we have recently read of Aldous Huxley's enjoyment of a newly vital and colourful perception of objects under the influence of mescalin, his adventure closely repeating the many examples reported by William James as the results of mystical experience in his *Varieties of Religious Experience*. But what Murry received through a single, shattering insight which did not prove permanent and Huxley has known through drugs, Powys in his fascinating book *In Spite Of* (1953) regards as achievable by all of us through a deliberate, psychic technique constituting the first step of an evolutionary advance in human consciousness. The statement corresponds closely to that of Wordsworth's well-known *Recluse* fragment, as published in the Preface to *The Excursion*.

This perception lies at the heart of *A Glastonbury Romance*; and since this book is also the heart of Powys's work, a retrospective comment may prove helpful. Its opening, which includes a discussion of certain correspondences between solar activity and a human consciousness, has been regarded as a stumbling-block to the pusillanimous reader; and yet this is a deeply considered and necessary introduction. It is precisely Powys's ever-present contact with the vital, or spiritual, principles within the universe which enables him to explore with so uncanny a penetration the deeper problems of that comparatively small section of the universe—or, as he would say, multiverse—which constitutes man; and this is how his human delineation comes to register an advance on previous novelists, and even dramatists. *A Glastonbury Romance* is rooted firmly in its cosmic setting and more especially in the soil and vegetation of Somerset. Within this setting, and one with it, are the people. These are many, and the minor persons are drawn with as much sympathy as the greater: the gardener Weatherwax, Mad Bet, the boy Elphin Cantle, are as convincing as any such in Hardy or Shakespeare. But our, if not the author's, main interest falls inevitably on those in the centre; and here the range and depth of experience depicted is enormous. But again, it is only because Powys has as deep a sympathy for, and insight into, his ferns and funguses, his Mad Bets and Elphin Cantles, as in his sun or Grail or the First Cause itself, that he can handle the greater—if they are the greater—mysteries with such consummate ease.

Such an awareness of the magical, corresponding to what John Davidson in his introduction to *The Theatrocrat* (1905; 25) regarded as the *bisexual* electricity within phenomena, is likely to be peculiarly authoritative in the expression of sexual instincts. The chapter of *A Glastonbury Romance* headed 'Consummation' offers us probably as profound an insight into the willed submission of feminine love as we shall anywhere find; and here Powys may be contrasted with Lawrence, whose women appear so often to love with a male complexity which appears more characteristic of the author than of the female sex. No experienced reader of Powys will lack confidence in his human exploitations, however strange the adventures; and in *A Glastonbury Romance* we meet one of the strangest and most terrifying studies in fiction—the sadistic Mr Evans.

Mr Evans is a lovable, academically minded man with a fondness for old Welsh manuscripts but tormented by a recurring sadistic obsession utterly at variance with his better nature. It is not—apart from one suggestion of a pre-natal incident (XXIX, 1068 or 1020)—handled as a 'perversion', attributable to some fault in upbringing or character; rather is Mr Evans's sexual mechanism shown as directly reflecting and responding to that side of the creative process, or great 'First Cause', which is responsible for the manifest cruelties of the cosmic scheme.

On the human plane, we must search for ways to escape; and two ways are suggested. First, Mr Evans tries to conquer the evil by acting the part of the crucified Christ in a Passion Play, with the inevitably suggested corollary that it is this particular instinct, as a universal problem in man and in nature, which lies behind both the necessity and the power of Christian symbolism. Second, Mr Evans's pathetically plain wife pits the dubious, and yet partly successful, charms of her own body against her husband's evil possession.

Beside the evil we have the good. Growing naturally from Powys's spiritual, or magical, apprehensions, Glastonbury is shown to us as a spot uniquely open to what T.S. Eliot has called the 'intersection of the timeless with time'. Those poignant intimations of the *Four Quartets* are here found massively and realistically expanded for us in direct descent from the main mythological traditions of our island: there is little arbitrary, or personal, in the treatment, which feels myth as objectively and potently active as any beast or tree; as part, indeed, of nature itself. Two persons in the book attain a semi-transcendental stature: the miracle-working and ghost-exorcizing Mr Geard, and the saintly Sam. These studies are the more convincing in that they are done without any touch of idealism. Mr Geard's religious phraseology is that of a peculiarly crude revivalist. As for Sam, his vision of the Grail comes directly before he has to minister—and we are spared no physical detail—to an old man suffering from piles. In line with the great traditions of Christian sanctity, we are forced to buy our visions at the price of what is humanly repellent. Nor must we forget that there is throughout a Rabelaisian humour. But this in no sense lowers the theme. Rabelais, of whom he has published a notable study, is one of Powys's own most persistent influences; and his most searching analyses are habitually given with ironic detachment and a play of humour.

A Glastonbury Romance was a great act of courage; and Powys's *Autobiography* (1934), in which he claims to recognize the presence of the sadistic instinct within himself, was an even greater. The power of *A Glastonbury Romance* matures from its controlled survey of good and evil as balanced and artistically accepted principles within the universe and within man. This acknowledged, we may next suggest that Powys's genius, his extraordinarily wide and deep comprehension of human instincts and potentialities, derives from his own intimate experience of a terrible evil; through accepting without surrendering to it he has gained an inclusiveness known to few in immediate contact with the origins, beyond good and evil, of creation. And surely, it is this very acceptance, as an intimate and personal experience, of the deepest and most fearful cleavage and antagonism of opposing principles within and yet intrinsic to the cosmic scheme, which enables him so uncannily to focus the secret life of sticks and stones, recognizing in them what theologians would call the immanence of the Deity.

This dispassionate balancing of good and evil, and in particular the evils of cruelty, could scarcely be, on all occasions, maintained. When an evil is too pressingly known, there is also the compulsion on the artist to descend into the arena, to fight; and for many years Powys has engaged himself strenuously against his main horror, vivisection. This campaign found its most satisfying projection in *Morwyn* (1937), a richly compacted 'Inferno' where, among others, the majestic figures of Taliessin and Merlin appear as powers of good.

The novels of Welsh history, *Owen Glendower* (1942) and *Porius* (1951), completed Powys's weightier works. Since those appeared we have been aware of an easier, more buoyant manner in the Homeric *Atlantis* (1954) and medieval *The Brazen Head* (1956). These later books take us directly to a world of myth and enchantment which allows a new freedom in the handling of the animistic properties of nature, as in the delightfully argumentative Fly and Moth of *Atlantis* and the parts played, in both narratives, by certain peculiarly wise trees. The importance of these lively creations was well emphasized recently by Mr Roland Mathias in a valuable broadcast.

Cosmic Correspondences

And here we are brought to the threshold of the two new stories published under the title *Up and Out*.

We have Powys's own authority for regarding the animistic insight as their key; but this is not necessarily a happy insight. It is just because he makes no distinction between the sensitivities of animals and men that his horror of vivisection is so great. The first story opens with an attack on this recurring horror, in comparison with which the subsequent brief and unsensational announcement that the world has just been destroyed by atomic warfare comes, with a typical stroke of Powysian idiosyncrasy, as an anti-climax. Four survivors voyage on a fragment of Earth into space. The fantastic adventure shows us the slaying of Time, conceived as an amorphous slug, and its swallowing by Eternity, an even more repellent creature which next swallows itself. The stars, through Aldebaran as representative, elect to commit general suicide. Representatives of Oriental, Greek, and Welsh mythology and religion accompany these remarkable events by argument and comment. Finally the four survivors meet God and Satan in friendly colloquy, after the manner of Goethe's *Faust*, and hear God's personal account of the creation which has proved so disastrous and his plan for a new attempt without either animal slaughter or free-will. The book's hero suggests instead that they all—God, Satan and the four survivors from Earth—attempt a plunge 'up and out' into the new 'dimension' sometimes discussed by philosophers. The attempt is made, but it leads only to extinction for all concerned.

The story constitutes an attack not only on vivisection

Cosmic Correspondences

and the lust for scientific knowledge, but also on all avenues of escape offered by such abstract concepts as 'eternity', 'dimension' and 'the Absolute', or any fixed theology. And yet the apparent pessimism is countered by so irrepressibly bouyant a style and so lively a play of humour that it can scarcely be regarded as final. The characterization of God is particularly attractive and entertaining. Never was there a more well-intentioned deity: simple-minded, unpretentious, courteous, kindly, indeed wholly lovable, and, like the God of Connolly's *Green Pastures*, surprisingly convincing. It almost seems as though Powys is nowadays at his happiest when speaking through the voice either of God himself or of some insect or inanimate object.

The two narratives are published, and may have been conceived, as complementary; certainly they should be read together, like the 'Everlasting No' and 'Everlasting Yea' of *Sartor Resartus*. The second [*The Mountains of the Moon*] is by far the happier. This fantasy takes us to the Moon, and is filled by heterogeneous persons and events moving with a dreamlike inconsequence which yet holds together as a pleasing unit. Among its constituent elements are some exciting meditations on the mystery of life, a stick in telepathic communication with a club, and a Moon-giant who possesses a collection of 'Milestones of Terrestial History', including a fragment of the Ten Commandments, Achilles' heel, Nero's fiddle-string, a white feather from the Dove of the Ark, a piece of one of King Alfred's burnt cakes, the half-bitten apple-core from Eden. Among the Moon-dwellers we find an academically minded and clairvoyant spinster and her friend, a professional, but baffled, philosopher; and from Earth we have a Welsh lady whose soul visits the Moon's soul in sleep. A romantic conclusion shows us the young hero, successor to the young heroes of *Atlantis* and *The Brazen Head*, climbing 'up and up and up' to find union with the daughter of the Moon and Sun on the ridge of the Moon's mountains which divides its known from its unknown face.

The fantasy, carried in a style of purity and charm, is wholly pleasing. The mysteries of 'space' and 'infinity' are metaphysical positives coming under no such condemnation as did 'time', 'eternity', and 'the Absolute' in the previous tale; indeed, the contrast is stated. Most vivid of all is the dance of the Terrestial Milestones and the characterization of the Dove's White Feather as she finds union with her long-lost love, a Raven's Black Feather from the Raven which did not, according to the account in Genesis, return to the Ark. No person of fiction was ever created with more masterly a touch, nor more warmly convincing in life and speech, than this fascinating White Feather. A few pages only, but the miracle is performed. Again, a line or two and a few scattered phrases endue a piece of quartz dancing 'ecstatically' down a slope with a lovable, semi-human vivacity surely new to our literature.

Here rather than in Powys's denials lies his true genius, and its meaning for us today. Rationally, he has always maintained a certain agnosticism; and yet each book in turn is saturated in a sense of the occult, of magic, of some hinterland to the phenomenal world of prodigious strangeness and importance. In his latest work this divergence appears to be widening. The uncompromising repudiation of immortality throughout *In Spite Of* stands in firm contrast to the range of possibility beyond death surveyed in his earlier book *Mortal Strife* (1942). Again and again he now urges us, just as did Wordsworth in the *Recluse* fragment and John Davidson in many an impassioned paragraph, to transfer finally our more numinous speculations from the altar to the earth, to the observable universe and all its children. And yet the more uncompromising his religious scepticism becomes, the more his narratives are charged with a sense of the miraculous. Perhaps he would say that when once we have touched the living magic of creation, then all the rest, our immortalities and eternities and dimensions and theologies, will be handed back to us, if we still want them; but not till then. In *The Mountains of the Moon* the hero, Rorlt, told by his faithful club, Blob, to 'listen', hears the still, sad music, not merely of man, but of the whole creation, understanding

> that there was some mysterious harmony in the souls of us all, in the souls of animals, vegetables and minerals, in the souls of water, air, earth, and fire, only, as Shakespeare says 'whilst this muddy vesture of decay doth grossly close it in we cannot hear it'—yes, that weird procession he had just heard and seen, of forms that were indistinguishable from the shapes created in the mind by tragic music when it transcends all particular sorrow and goes beyond all personal grief and is full of a strange sadness that all nature feels ... (208)

But now this tragic music, the central theme of so many of Powys's philosophical discussions, must itself be surpassed:

I

Cosmic Correspondences

It struck him as a revelation of something, but of something that it was essential for him to pass by, pass over, to shake off, to leave behind.

So the young Rorlt goes on to his union with Helia, while his trusty club, symbol of what we call the 'inanimate', slithers back, on *this* side of the ridge. Presumably this 'shaking off' includes the surmounting of all the cruelties and voracities of nature and perhaps even the vivisections, sadisms and atomic warring of men; and perhaps it is not fantastic to see in the poignant love-intercourse of our White and Black Feathers some delicate intimation, some feather-light whisper, hinting an answer. If so, it is an answer which Powys has not as yet explicitly formulated. His latest fantasy moves in advance of the main body of his teaching.

Appendix 2

15th January 1959

To the Nobel Committee of the Swedish Academy

This letter is written in reply to your kind request for a nomination for the Nobel Prize in Literature. I wish to nominate Mr John Cowper Powys. I enclose a number of papers in support. Most of these I had by me, and some I have procured from Messrs Macdonald. Mr Powys does not know anything about this nomination.

I have followed Mr Powys's work carefully for twenty-five years, and have never wavered in my opinion of its importance. In my published works I have recorded this opinion often, referring to *A Glastonbury Romance* in a book of 1939 as 'perhaps the greatest literary work of our generation'. Mr Powys's creative genius appears to be inexhaustible; and his contribution, often under severe difficulties, involving both ill-health and financial anxiety, has been heroic. Every one of his works projects the spirit of boundless goodwill as well as profundity; and humour too. There is something saintly about him. I think that he will be regarded in the future as one of the truly great names in our literature.

Mr Powys belongs to no particular literary school, to no rigid sect either of politics or religion. He is a great individualist of both mystical and realistic, even homely, understanding. He has been quite untainted by twentieth century defeatism: and perhaps because of this the literary middle men, the 'intelligentsia', have not always given his work the publicity it should have had, at least in England. It has, however, won its way through without that help. Not that there has been any doubt; there have been at least two valuable studies published of Mr Powys and his brothers: *The Powys Brothers*, by R.H. Ward, 1935; and *Welsh Ambassadors*, by Louis Marlow, 1936. The response particularly of creative writers has been wholehearted: among the papers enclosed you will see quotations from such well-known authors as Hugh Walpole, Sir Gerald Barry, J.D. Beresford and Angus Wilson. The novelist and dramatist, J.B. Priestley, has recently paid a tribute to his genius in a review. He has a strong following among the younger modern poets such as John Heath-Stubbs and Stevie Smith, whose comments you will find among the enclosed extracts. His work has been, or is being, translated into French, German and Japanese. His own literary commentaries, as published in *The Pleasures of Literature* and *Visions and Revisions*, have ranged widely over the world's literature, including the *Bible*, the Greeks, Dante, Rabelais, Cervantes, Goethe and Dostoievsky. In 1958 Mr Powys was the first foreigner to be awarded the Plaque of the Free Academy of Arts in Hamburg for 1957, being the third to receive this honour, succeeding Thomas Mann and the composer Ilse Fromm-Michaels.

During the early years of this century Mr Powys lectured widely on literature throughout the United States of America. He has a large following there, and was a friend of Theodore Dreiser. For many years now he has lived in Wales. He is himself partly of Welsh descent, and has often written as its national voice, using Welsh themes. He is saturated in both classical and Welsh mythology.

Were the Nobel Prize awarded to Mr Powys this would be, in my opinion, not only a fine and deserved tribute to a literary genius of fifty years outstanding activity, but, since Mr Powys is the eldest and only surviving writer of the most distinguished literary family of the century in Great Britain, a family which included T.F. Powys and Llewelyn Powys, men of high literary distinction, and A.R. Powys, the writer on architecture, it would be also an indirect tribute to this remarkable family as a whole.

Should you wish to correspond directly with people of literary standing who know and value Mr Powys's contribution I should be happy to make suggestions, or

Letter to the Nobel Committee

write to them myself, but it may be that you will not require such additional corroboration.

A representative selection of Mr Powys's books available at present is given on the inside cover of the magazine *New Chapter*. To this I should add Mr Powys's *Autobiography*, published by John Lane The Bodley Head. The rest of his work is handled by Messrs Macdonald & Co. If possible I should like the material which I am submitting to be returned to me eventually; but for this there is no hurry whatsoever.

G. Wilson Knight
Professor of English Literature

Appendix 3

Psychic News

London, 27 July 1963   No. 1625
World-famous writer returns to scholar

It was not surprising that John Cowper Powys, one of the greatest writers of his day, should return to prove his survival to a leading scholar who had paid public homage to him.

The spirit presence of Powys, a month after his passing, was described to G. Wilson Knight, former Professor of English Literature at Leeds University, who was attending a Spiritualist church in Exeter a few days ago. The visiting clairvoyant, Miss F. Horsfield of Bideford, Devon, told Knight that all through the service she had seen this figure standing by him.

'He is no relative,' she said. 'He passed over not long ago'—he died on June 17. When she described his 'rather gaunt features, high cheek bones and unruly hair,' the recipient thought that it might be Powys and awaited further details.

'He is a personality,' said the medium, who added that she found it difficult to get close to him. 'He was an occultist,' she went on, 'and knew as much as anyone about the continuity of life.'

Here Knight said that he knew Powys was an occultist, but he was not sure about the rest of the message. 'He wrote, didn't he?' asked the medium. Receiving the reply, 'Yes,' she inquired, 'Can I go to Wales?'

This made Knight sure that it was Powys communicating, for the last years of his earthly life were spent in Wales. Miss Horsfield said that Powys was so close to the recipient—'It's a wonder you can't sense him yourself.'

She referred to his powerful presence, adding, 'He is thanking you for what you did for him and in return he wants to help you.'

Knight has devoted a lot of his own literary attention to Powys and has in preparation a study of him.

Last October, on the occasion of Powys' 90th birthday, he wrote in the *Yorkshire Post* a three-column tribute in which he described him as 'the finest historical novelist in English literature and our greatest nature-writer.' Meeting him, he said, was 'to draw strength from a spiritual giant.' His work was 'done with the insight of a seer.'

It is no wonder that Powys chose this opportunity of returning to Knight through the medium. He indicated his awareness of the forthcoming study of him by saying that he was very interested in 'something you are going to do shortly.'

Knight was intrigued when the medium relayed the message. 'He says he will go with you.' At the end of this month he is visiting Canada for a few weeks to lecture on literary matters.

Once again the medium said that he was so strong an influence and such a wonderful personality that it was a job for her to break away from him. Then she commented on his lovely smile and described his characteristic mouth. The message ended with thanks 'for all your thought for him.'

Later Knight approached the medium to express his gratitude and to tell her who the communicator was. He mentioned that he regarded Powys as the greatest writer of our time and had written a good deal about him.

He added that Powys was always discussing the afterlife in book after book and had a vast occult understanding, but at the end he was doubtful about personal survival. The medium replied that anyway he knew about it now.

She volunteered that she had not read any of his works. Miss Horsfield repeated several times that the power accompanying this communication was beyond anything she had experienced. It was all she could do to prevent herself being controlled by him.

Knight tells us that Powys had direct experience of astral travel and throughout most of his life insisted on

Major Publications by Powys and Knight

the limitations of our ordinary perceptions. He sent out thoughts of what he called 'coloured angels' to heal people and animals.*

Appendix 4

Major Publications by
John Cowper Powys and G. Wilson Knight
During the Period covered by this Correspondence
1932-1962

For full bibliographies see Derek Langridge's *John Cowper Powys, A Record of Achievement*, London, 1966; Dante Thomas's *A Bibliography of the Writings of John Cowper Powys: 1872-1963*, Mamaroneck (N.Y.), 1975; and 'A Select List of the Published Writings of George Wilson Knight', compiled by John E. van Domelen and appended to *The Morality of Art, Essays Presented to G. Wilson Knight by his Colleagues and Friends*, edited by D.W. Jefferson, London, 1969.

Powys	Knight
1932 *A Glastonbury Romance*	*The Shakespearian Tempest*
1933 *A Philosophy of Solitude*	*The Christian Renaissance*
1934 *Weymouth Sands* (*Jobber Skald* in England, 1935)	
Autobiography	
1935 *The Art of Happiness*	

---

*Later Miss Horsfield received the word 'sensualism' as additional Powys evidence. See *Neglected Powers*, 'Mysticism and Masturbation', p. 164, note.—G.W.K.

Major Publications by Powys and Knight

Powys	Knight
1936 Maiden Castle	Principles of Shakespearian Production (revised in 1964 as Shakespearian Production)
	Atlantic Crossing
1937 Morwyn	
1938 The Pleasures of Literature (The Enjoyment of Literature in America)	
1939	The Burning Oracle
1941 Owen Glendower	The Starlit Dome
1942 Mortal Strife	Chariot of Wrath
1944 The Art of Growing Old	The Olive and the Sword
1945	The Dynasty of Stowe
1946	Hiroshima
1947 Dostoievsky	The Crown of Life
Obstinate Cymric	
1948 Rabelais	Christ and Nietzsche
1951 Porius	
1952 The Inmates	Lord Byron: Christian Virtues
1953 In Spite Of	
1954 Atlantis	The Last of the Incas
	Laureate of Peace
1955	The Mutual Flame
1956 Lucifer	
The Brazen Head	
1957 Up and Out	Lord Byron's Marriage
1958 The Letters of John Cowper Powys to Louis Wilkinson: 1935-1956	The Sovereign Flower
1959 Homer and the Aether	
1960 All or Nothing	
1962	The Golden Labyrinth
	Ibsen

Index

Aberystwyth College 75
Achilles 36, 83, 85, 93
Aeneid 60, 114n
All or Nothing (Powys) 17, 99, 106
Almanac (J.R. Anderson) 62, 91
America 8, 13, 77, 113n, 132
Anderson, Gweneth (Mrs John Redwood Anderson) 91
Anne, Queen 102
Antony 101
Antony and Cleopatra 26
Apollo 93
Ariel 101
Aristophanes 36, 37, 41
Aristotle 60
Arnold, Matthew 14, 55
Arthur, King 75
Art of Growing Old (Powys) 71
Aspasia 84
Athene, Pallas 41, 72
Athens 50
Atlantic Crossing (Knight) 25, 29, 30
Atlantis (Powys) 125, 128
Augustus, Emperor 86
Autobiography (Powys) 7, 9, 14, 16, 17, 21, 27, 36, 57, 124, 132
Aztecs 120

Bacon, Roger 49, 50
Barnes, William 104, 115n
Barrie, Sir Gerald 131
Basilisk of St James (E. Myers) 59
Bath 63
Bennett, Arnold 54
Beresford, J.D. 131
Berry, Francis 11, 31, 33, 44, 86, 111n
Bible 36, 70, 132
Big Sur, California 50
Birth of Tragedy (Nietzsche) 14, 102
Blackburn, Tom 91
Blaenau Ffestiniog 52, 57, 59, 70-71
Blake, William 14, 119
Bluebeard 70
Bodley Head 45, 133
Boleyn, Anne 89
'Book on Drama' or 'Drama Book' see *The Golden Labyrinth* (G. Wilson Knight)
Boston 47
Brazen Head (Powys) 49, 59, 61, 62, 91, 125, 128
Browning, Robert 96
Brussels 68
Burning Oracle (Knight) 325
Byron, Lord 10, 11, 41, 65, 66, 107, 119
'Byron's Book', see *Lord Byron's Marriage* (Knight)

Caliban 26, 27, 28n, 101
Cambridge University 13, 107
Campion, Oliver 70, 98, 104
Canada 8, 12, 135
Canavaggia, Marie 115n
Carlyle, Thomas 119
Cassell 33
Cervantes 132
Ceylon 96, 97, 98
Chaucer, G. 76
Cheltenham 25
Christ 33, 34, 51, 70, 94
Christian Renaissance (Knight) 25, 29, 36
City of Dreadful Night (James Thomson, 'B.V.') 81
Clark Lectures 107
Cleopatra 101
Colman, George 66
Connolly, Cyril 127
Coriolanus 101

INDEX

Corpus Christi, Cambridge 8, 77
Cowper, William 70
Craig, Gordon 100
Cromwell, Oliver 86

Daily Telegraph 78
Dante 47, 60, 86, 132
Davidson, John 81, 84, 119, 122, 129
Dean Close School, Cheltenham 11-12
De la Mare, Walter 52
de Montfort, Simon 50
De Quincey, Thomas 69
De Retz, Gilles 70
Dickens, Charles 47
Dock Leaves 114n
Donne, John 89
Don Leon (Byron) 66
Dorothy M. Richardson (Powys) 13
Dorset 8, 104, 106, 107, 112n
Dostoievsky (Powys) 13
Dostoievsky, F.M. 34, 48, 132
Dreiser, Theodore 51, 132
Dulwich College 11

Ecclesiastical Polity (R. Hooker) 120
Egeria 84
Elia 81
Elijah 36
Eliot, T.S. 123
Elizabeth I 102
Elwin, Malcolm 111n
Essay on Man (Pope) 26
Essays in Criticism 115n, 116n
Essays on John Cowper Powys (ed. B. Humfrey) 112n
Etruscans 120
Excursion (Wordsworth) 121
Exeter 79, 92, 94
Exeter University 96

Fall of a Tower (F. Berry) 31
Falstaff 47
Faust (Marlowe) 86
Faust (Goethe) 86, 103, 126

'For John Cowper Powys on his Ninetieth Birthday' (sonnet by F. Berry) 111-112n
Fouqué, Baron de la Motte 75
Four Quartets (T.S. Eliot) 123
Frankenstein 88
Fromm-Michaels, Ilse 132

Galloping Centaur (F. Berry) 111n
Garlick, Raymond 76, 114n
Ghost of Greenland (F. Berry) 111n
Glastonbury Romance (Powys) 8, 25, 26, 27, 29, 38, 119, 121-124, 131
God (J.M. Murry) 121
Goethe, J.W. von 65, 86, 103, 126, 132
Golden Labyrinth (Knight) 70, 74, 76, 87, 88, 89, 97, 104, 107, 108
Green Pastures (C. Connolly) 127
Greenwood, Mr 45
Gregory, Alyse 92
Grimm's Fairy Tales 70
Guest, Lady Charlotte 74, 75, 76, 92

Ham 90
Hamburg 98, 99
Hanley, James 50
Hara, Ichiro 97, 115n
Hardy, Thomas 104, 115n, 116n, 122
Harvey, Eric 82, 106
Hawthorne, Nathaniel 77
Hazlitt, William 84
Heath-Stubbs, John 52, 131
Hector 36, 93
Henry VIII (Shakespeare) 99
Henry III 49, 50
Hera 92
Hermes 93
Hobhouse, John 66
Homer 36, 60, 65, 87, 92, 125
Homer and the Aether (Powys) 60, 73, 99, 104
Hooker, Richard 120

Horace 86, 100
Horsefield, F. 133-5
Houghton, Claude 51
Hound of Heaven (F. Thompson) 118-9
Hull University 91
Huxley, Aldous 121

Ibsen, H. 107
Iliad 60, 85, 86-87, 92, 99
Inmates (Powys) 42
In Spite Of (Powys) 121, 129
Irving, Henry 100
Italiaander, Rolf 99
I Tell of Greenland (F. Berry) 112n

Jackson Knight: a Biography (G. Wilson Knight) 12
Jack the Ripper 69, 70
James, Henry 7
James, William 51, 121
Japan 96, 97, 98, 115n
Jerusalem 50
Jobber Skald (English ed., 1935, of *Weymouth Sands*, New York; Powys) 76, 115, 119
John, Augustus 98
John, King 50
John Cowper Powys: a Record of Achievement (D. Langridge) 112n
John Cowper Powys: Letters to Glyn Hughes (ed. B. Jones) 115n
Johnson, Mrs Barham (Powys's cousin Catharine) 89
Jones, Bernard 104, 115n
Jones, Glyn 75
Jonson, Ben 88
Joyce, James 7, 8, 107, 118
Judas 94

Kansas City 47
Kant, I. 63
Karl August, Emperor 86
Keats, John 32, 102
Kenya 59, 107

Knight, Caroline (mother of G. Wilson Knight) 11, 38, 43
Knight, George (father of G. Wilson Knight) 11
Knight, G. Wilson: his piercing eyes 10, 56, 59, 60, 65, 81; his works on Shakespeare, Pope, Byron, the Romantic poets and British drama 11; autobiographical writing of 11; nominates Powys for Nobel Prize 11, 95, 130-33; précis of his life 11-12; four meetings with Powys 12-13; similarities with Powys 13, 20, 62; interest in the occult 12, 13, 56, 65; essentially an actor 13, 14, 26, 27, 28, 61, 62; Nietzsche's influence on 14, 15; as an exhibitionist 16, 26, 27, 28, 61; his initiation of the correspondence 25, 27, 29; his one-man dramatic recital 28n; his first visit to Powys 35, 36, 37; dedicates *Laureate of Peace* to Powys 38-39, 45, 46, 53; his second visit to Powys 54, 55; writings on Powys's work 58, 59-60, 61, 73-4, 78, 79, 80, 86, 96, 104, 106, 107, 117-133; his third visit to Powys 64, 68, 69, 70, 71, 72; remarks on masturbation 71; remarks on sex 92; on the possible publication of his letters from Powys 117; Powys's posthumappearance to 133-36
Knight, Mr (of Impington) 44, 77
Knight, Philippa (godmother and relation of Powys) 77, 112n
Knight, W.F. Jackson 12, 36, 37, 58, 112n, 114n
Koran 70
Kwintner, Jeffrey 95

Lamb, Charles 81
Lancaster, Robert V. 114n
Langridge, Derek 112n

INDEX

Last of the Incas (Knight) 51, 113n
Laureate of Peace (Knight) 38, 45, 46, 112n, 113n
Lawrence, D.H. 7, 8, 20, 107, 116n, 118, 119, 120, 122
Lear, King 28n
Leeds University 12
Letters to Llewelyn Powys (Powys) 111n
Letters to Louis Wilkinson (Powys) 98
Lily 69
Living Universe (F. Younghusband) 120
Lord Byron's Marriage (Knight) 10, 41, 57, 64, 65, 66, 67, 71
Love and Death (Llewelyn Powys) 45
Lovelace, Richard 66
Lucifer (Powys) 57, 58, 60, 61, 119
Lulworth 80
Lyon, Harry 90, 113n
Lyon, Margaret (Powys's wife) 48, 51, 69, 113n

Mabinogion (ed. C. Guest) 74, 75, 92, 96, 120
Macdonald & Co. 59, 75, 82, 85, 91, 99, 106, 108, 130, 133
Madoc, Prince 97
Magna Carta 50
Mann, Thomas 132
Marie Louise, Princess 80
Marlow, Louis (*pseud.* Louis Wilkinson) 131
Marlowe, Christopher 86
Masters, Edgar Lee 51
Mathias, Roland 125
Matthews (Dean of Winchester) 85
Meaning of Culture (Powys) 8, 96, 98, 115n
Merlin 75, 125
Miller, Henry 7, 50
Milton, John 86, 100
Mr. Weston's Good Wine (T.F. Powys) 113n
Mithras 75

Moral Essays (Pope) 26
Morant Bay (F. Berry) 111n
Mortal Strife (Powys) 129
Morwyn (Powys) 125
Mother Goose 70
Motwani, Kewal 96, 97, 98
Mountains of the Moon (Powys) 117, 127-30
Munich 75
Murry, J. Middleton 48, 121
Myers, Elizabeth 59, 62
Myth and Miracle (Knight) 11

Napoleon 76
Nasser, Col. 57, 60
National Museum of Wales 75
Neglected Powers (Knight) 11, 26, 27, 28, 111n, 112n, 113n, 117
New Chapter 95, 96, 133
Nietzsche, F.W. 14, 15, 26, 27, 28, 33, 34, 47, 51, 56, 102
Nietzsche, Frau Foster 77

Observer 73
Odysseus 73
O'Casey, Sean 101
O'Neill, Eugene 101
Owen Glendower (Powys) 125
Oxford University 13

Panurge 36
Paris 63, 68
Pasithea 92
Patroclus 83
Patterson, Dr 39
Philosophy of Solitude (Powys) 115n
Philpotts, Eden 89
Phoenix 85
Phoenix House 85
Pius XII, Pope 103
Plato 60
Playter, Phyllis *throughout*
Pleasures of Literature [*Enjoyment of Literature*] (Powys) 14, 30, 132
Plon 76
Poems of William Barnes (ed. B.

141

Jones) 115n
Pope, Alexander 11, 38, 45, 51, 53, 102
Porius (Powys) 9, 20, 41, 42, 75, 125
Powys, Albert Reginald (brother) 98, 111n, 132
Powys, Charles Francis (father) 8, 52-3, 73, 77, 104, 111n
Powys, Isobel (niece) 98
Powys, John Cowper: précis of life 7-8; prolific letterwriter 11; nominated for Nobel Prize 11, 95, 130-33; four meetings with Knight 13, 20, 62; interest in the first cause 13; essentially an actor 13, 14, 34, 61, 62; Nietzsche's influence on 14, 15; his sadistic obsession 16, 26, 57-8, 61, 63, 64, 66, 67, 68, 80, 81, 83; and masturbation 16-20, 63, 68, 69; his 'anti-narcissism' 33, 34, 61, 62, 114n; on humility 34, 47; Knight's first visit 35, 36, 37; his attitude to his brothers Llewelyn, Theodore and Littleton 37; concern with bodily functions 38, 39, 40; his vegetarian diet 38, 40, 41; on Knight's failure to receive full recognition 42-3; on the mystery of names 43; on cremation 43; on Knight's literary work 46, 47, 51, 91, 100-103, 104; on conceit 46; on the lies of history 50; moves to Blaenau Ffestiniog 52; his admiration for Walter de la Mare 52; Knight's second visit 54, 55; his craving to invent and recite 62; his relationship with his son 63, 67-8; his loss of sexual excitement 63, 66, 68; on his lack of 'the passion of love' 63; his vain attempt to become a homosexual 67; Knight's third visit 64, 68-9, 70, 71, 72; on the understanding between the old and the very young 71-2; on the Welsh language 76; on modern poetry 84; longs for annihilation 88, 89; on the feminine principle 103; on the Church 103; horror of vivisection 125, 126-27; posthumous appearance to Knight 133-136

Powys, Littleton Charles (grandfather) 44, 53, 67, 77, 112n
Powys, Littleton Charles (brother) 37, 49, 55, 59, 61, 62, 80, 113n
Powys, Mrs Littleton C. (grandmother) 112n
Powys, Llewelyn ('Lulu'; brother) 9, 17, 18, 23, 37, 45, 73, 83, 90, 91, 92, 111n, 132
Powys, Margaret (wife) 48, 51, 69, 113n
Powys, Marian (sister) 111n
Powys, Mary Cowper (mother) 8, 96, 100
Powys, Philippa ('Katie'; sister) 107
Powys, Theodore Francis (brother) 37, 48, 96, 98, 113n, 132
Powys, William (brother) 59, 90, 107
Powys Brothers (R.H. Ward) 131
Powys Newsletter 111n, 115n
Priam 93
Priestley, J.B. 131
Prometheus Unbound (Shelley) 119
Prospero 87, 101
Psychic News 117, 133-6
Purdy, James 73

Rabelais (Powys) 13, 50, 112n, 124
Rabelais, F. 47, 52, 124, 132
Recluse (Wordsworth) 121, 129
Review of English Literature 95
Review of English Studies 114n
Robeson, Paul 79
Roman Vergil (W.F.J. Knight) 33, 112n

INDEX

Romer Mowl and Other Stories (Powys; ed. B. Jones) 115n
Ruthin Castle Clinic 39

St Anne 85
St Edmund Hall, Oxford 11
Sartor Resartus (Carlyle) 119, 127
Saturnian Quest (Knight) 11
'Scholar Gipsy' (Arnold) 11, 14, 55
Seasons (J. Thomson) 81
Seeley, Prof. 60
Seymour, William Kean 51
Shakespeare, William 7, 11, 12, 47, 61, 74, 87, 99, 100, 101-2, 122, 129
Shakespearian Production (Knight) 12, 26, 28, 111n
Shakespeare's Dramatic Challenge (Knight) 28n
Shaw, G.B. 100, 101
Shelley, P.B. 119
Shelley, Mary Wollstonecraft 88
Sherborne 49, 57, 62, 80, 84
Shirley, Alice 73, 112n
Shirley, Ralph 77, 112n
Shirley, Walter Waddington 77, 112n
Sitwell, Edith 120
Sleep 92
Smith, Stevie 131
Somerset and Dorset Essays (L. Powys) 73
Sommers, Alan 76, 107, 115n
Sovereign Flower (Knight) 100, 103
Starlit Dome (Knight) 32
Steiner, George 116n
Sterne, Laurence 47
Still the Joy of It (Littleton Powys) 59, 61, 62
Stowe School 12
Sunday Times 67
Swift, Jonathan 49, 101
Symbol of Man (unpublished work; Knight) 14, 28

Taliessin 125

Tennyson, Alfred Lord 53, 76, 100, 102
Terry, Ellen 100
Tess of the D'Urbervilles 104
Theatrocrat (Powys) 122
Theodoric the Icelander (Baron de la Motte Fouqué) 75
This Sceptred Isle (Knight) 28
Thompson, Francis 81, 84, 118
Thomson, James 81
Thomson, James ('B.V.') 81
Thus Spake Zarathustra 26, 27, 28
Times 78
Times Literary Supplement 77, 78, 82, 96, 98, 104, 106, 107, 113n, 116n
Time Magazine 19
Timon 12, 26, 27, 34, 61, 62, 74, 101, 112n
Titus Andronicus 115n
Transatlantic Journey (Powys's title for Knight's *Atlantic Crossing*) 29
Trinity College, Toronto 12
Turner, Margaret 106
Twentieth Century 60, 104

Undine (Baron de la Motte Fouqué) 75
'Ulysses' (Tennyson) 53
Up and Out (Powys) 73, 78, 79, 117-27

Varieties of Religious Experience (W. James) 121
Vedanta 70
Victoria, Queen 13, 102
Village Press, London 8, 95
Virgil 58
Virgin Mary 85, 103
Visions and Revisions (Powys) 132

Wade, Rosalind 51
Wales 8, 23
Walpole, Hugh 131
Ward, R.H. 131
Well Full of Leaves (E. Myers) 59

Welsh Ambassadors (L. Marlow) 131
Westminster Theatre, London 28
Wheel of Fire (Knight) 11
White, John Foster 85
Whitman, Walt 84
Wildman, W.B. 84
Wilkinson, Joan 83
Wilkinson, Louis 9, 10, 23, 64, 83, 96, 98, 114n, 131; *see also* Marlow, L.
Wilson, Angus 7, 131
Wilson, Tommy 53
Winchester, Marquis of 88
Wolf Solent (Powys) 8, 16, 25, 106

Wood and Stone (Powys) 106, 120
Wordsworth, William 119, 121, 129
Wrexham Hospital 39

Yeats, J.B. (father of W.B. Yeats) 77
Yeats, W.B. 77, 84, 115n
York, Archbishop of 85
Yorkshire Post 61, 62, 104, 115n, 134
Younghusband, Sir Francis 120

Zeus 93, 98